Making Parish Councils PASTORAL

Mark F. Fischer

Paulist Press
New York/Mahwah, NJ

Author photo on back cover by John Lewis
Cover design by Sharyn Banks
Book design by Lynn Else

Library of Congress Cataloging-in-Publication Data

Fischer, Mark F.
    Making parish councils pastoral / Mark F. Fischer.
        p. cm.
    Includes bibliographical references (p.   ) and index.
    ISBN 978-0-8091-4676-5 (alk. paper)
    1. Parish councils. 2. Catholic Church—Government. 3. Pastoral theology—Catholic Church. I. Title.
    BX1920.F575 2010
    254´.02—dc22

                                                                2010019561

Published by Paulist Press
997 Macarthur Boulevard
Mahwah, New Jersey 07430

www.paulistpress.com

Printed and bound in the
United States of America

Contents

Acknowledgments

Books are the products of shared wisdom. That is especially true for a book that purports to be about sharing wisdom in the pastoral council. Pastors consult councils because they seek wisdom. They understand that a decision is good for the Christian community when it reflects and expresses the community's wisdom. To the extent that this book is good, it reflects the wisdom of those who have shaped the author's thinking.

Included in that number are those who, in the Diocese of Oakland, California, first gave me an opportunity to work with pastoral councils: Most Rev. John S. Cummins; Rev. Joseph Carroll, SJ; Marcia Frideger, SNJM; and Rev. George E. Crespin.

Many in the Conference for Pastoral Planning and Council Development, good friends and excellent colleagues, have indirectly shaped my thinking about councils: Mary Kay Bailey, OP; Michael Cieslak; Arthur X. Deegan II; David DeLambo; Richard Krivanka; Robert J. Miller; Mary Montgomery, OP; Mary Margaret Raley; and Loughlan Sofield, ST.

In the Archdiocese of Los Angeles, I am fortunate to serve as professor under Msgr. Craig Cox, rector of St. John's Seminary, and to serve with my colleagues in the pastoral council ministry, David Estrada, Anita Ford, Cambria Smith, and Maria Elena Uribe.

My writing about councils has benefited from the critical scrutiny of the following members of the academy: Rev. James A. Coriden, Bryan T. Froehle, Bradford E. Hinze, Mary L. Gautier, and Charles E. Zech.

I am especially grateful to the pastors who allowed their stories to be published in this book: Father James Stehly, pastor of St. Mary Magdalen Church in Camarillo; Father Joseph Visperas (pastor) and Father Patrick Gannon (pastor emeritus), St. Paul of the Cross, La

Mirada; and Msgr Michael Bunny, pastor of St. Julie Billiart Church in Newbury Park.

Dan Connors, when he was editor of *Today's Parish* magazine, gave me a start in writing about councils. My son, David J. Fischer, has helped me with my Web site, www.pastoralcouncils.com. Father Michael Kerrigan, CSP, edited and improved this book, helping me to keep my thoughts about councils in print.

Introduction

Today, almost fifty years after the initial flowering of the Second Vatican Council, Catholics throughout the world are still of many minds regarding consultation through parish pastoral councils. Although such councils flourish in the majority of U.S. dioceses and parishes, nevertheless experts disagree about their origin and purpose. This book aims to resolve those two questions.

It argues that the pastoral council is a specific type of council first recommended in Vatican II's Decree on Bishops of 1965.[1] That decree viewed the pastoral council as the servant of the pastor's particular apostolate or mission. It serves that apostolate in a threefold way. Under the pastor's direction, the council investigates some practical aspect of the church's life, ponders it, and recommends its conclusions to the pastor. By accepting the council's recommendations, the pastor affirms the wisdom of the council. By implementing them, he allows the councillors' wisdom to influence his apostolate, the apostolate of pastoral leadership. This is the correct way to understand the pastoral council.

Understood this way, the pastoral council synthesizes two dimensions of the Christian tradition. One dimension, reflected in the tenth chapter of John's gospel, views the pastor as the Good Shepherd. The Good Shepherd says, "I know my own and my own know me" (John 10:14). This is knowledge, not just of individuals, but of the community's wisdom. The Good Shepherd who knows his own recognizes their prudence and practical wisdom. They acknowledge his leadership as pastor. This knowledge is the type that builds communion. Mutual knowledge leads to mutual commitment. That is the first dimension of the Christian tradition reflected in the Church's teaching about pastoral councils.

The second dimension is the tradition of Greek philosophy taken up into Christian thought. Greek philosophy recognized the

1

branch of knowledge we call "practical wisdom." Practical wisdom, Aristotle said, is the knowledge about how to act in a changing situation. Because the situation changes, one cannot gain that knowledge from a textbook. One can only gain it through a dialogue with knowledgeable people. The Church's teaching about the pastoral council builds upon this fundamentally Greek insight. Disciplined conversation leads to wisdom.

The Church's teaching about the pastoral council synthesizes the Johannine and the Greek traditions. Dialogue, a fundamentally Greek idea, is the method of the pastoral council. In dialogue, the partners become more aware of themselves. Pope Paul VI treated the concept of dialogue in his first encyclical, *Ecclesiam suam*.[2] He wrote that, by means of dialogue, the Church becomes more aware of itself and reforms itself. When priests and people discuss their common concerns, they better understand the Church and their own role in the drama of salvation. When we deepen our relationship with one another in dialogue, we deepen our relationship with God. The goal is that "there will be one flock, one shepherd" (John 10:16).

DIVERGENT VOICES

According to the idea of the pastoral council, the pastor consults his people. He invites them to engage with him in a process of study and reflection. The goal is a dialogue that will lead to wise conclusions, conclusions that the pastoral council will recommend to him. When he accepts the council's recommendations, he may implement them through the parish's professional staff or through volunteers. The volunteers may even include the councillors themselves. But when the councillors implement the recommendations they have made, they do so as volunteers, and not (strictly speaking) as members of the council. The council has a consultative-only vote. It is not an executive body that implements its recommendations through a system of standing committees.

Some disagree with this assertion, however. They maintain the thesis that the pastoral council is an executive body. They say that the council coordinates a system of committees or commissions.[3] The committees or commissions (e.g., liturgy, social justice, education, etc.) do the parish's work of ministry. The council coordinates them by setting policy and monitoring performance. It sets goals and objectives for the committees and commissions to meet. From this point of view, the executive role of the pastoral council is essential. If the pastoral council did not coordinate committees and commissions, some say, parish ministry would not happen.

The origin of this divergent point of view has a complicated history that will occupy a major part of this book. Briefly, those who hold it believe that the Vatican II Decree on the Laity[4] (and not the Decree on Bishops) is the real source for the parish pastoral council. The Laity Decree called for councils at a variety of levels, including the parish level. In fact, it contained the only reference to parish councils in the Vatican II documents. These councils were intended to assist the Church's apostolic work. The Laity Decree said that the councils could even take care of the mutual coordinating of lay associations and undertakings, provided they did not limit their autonomy. So the divergent point of view pinpoints the origin of the parish pastoral council in the Vatican II Laity Decree.

Those who hold the divergent view also seize upon the verb *to coordinate*. They apply this verb, taken from the Laity Decree, to parish pastoral councils. They argue that the verb gives to parish pastoral councils the right to coordinate parish committees and commissions. The proper understanding of the parish pastoral council, they say, is the one presented in the Laity Decree. The council assists the Church's apostolic work by coordinating a system of committees and commissions, according to this view, a system that performs the ministerial work of the parish. In short, the reference to "coordination" in the 1965 Laity Decree is the basis for the divergent viewpoint presented here.

THE PASTORAL VIEWPOINT

The present book is dedicated to the proposition that Vatican II did not intend parish pastoral councils to be the coordinators of a system of committees and commissions. The Laity Decree never mentioned "pastoral" councils. It is a mistake to regard that decree as their source. The Bishops Decree, the proper foundation for the pastoral council, did not give them the task of "coordination." It asked them to investigate, reflect, and propose conclusions to the pastor.

The proper task of the pastoral council is the search for wisdom, not the supervision of committees. The pastor consults the council for the sake of his own apostolate, the apostolate of church leadership. That was Vatican II's intention for the "pastoral" council.

From this viewpoint, it is the pastor—not the council—who coordinates ministerial groups. The pastor is the coordinator because the bishop has entrusted the parish to him. To be sure, he may coordinate the ministries of the parish as he sees fit. In this regard, the pastor has a lot of leeway. He may use a system of committees or commissions. He may even establish a coordinating committee composed of the representatives of each ministry.

Such a coordinating committee, however, is not a pastoral council. As defined in the Decree on Bishops, a pastoral council has a threefold task. Under the pastor's leadership, it investigates practical questions, reflects on them, and proposes to him its conclusions. He consults the council because he wants its help. He wants it to help him exercise the responsibility which, legally speaking, is his alone: the responsibility of pastoring the parish.

Those who regard the Decree on the Laity (with its references to councils that coordinate lay associations) as the basis for the pastoral council are mistaken. The proper basis is the Decree on Bishops. There we find the clearest and most coherent source for the pastoral council. Although not every Vatican document has unambiguously endorsed this understanding, not one has denied it, and the vast majority has lent it strong support. On the basis of the Bishops Decree, one can clearly state the identity and purpose of the pastoral council. On this basis, one can make a judgment about whether parish councils are truly pastoral.

HOW MY UNDERSTANDING HAS CHANGED

My understanding of the pastoral council has slightly changed since the publication in 2001 of *Pastoral Councils in Today's Catholic Parish*.[5] In that book, I was at pains to assert that Vatican II is a better and more comprehensive source for understanding parish pastoral councils than canon 536, the sole reference to them in the 1983 Code of Canon Law. Canon 536 was selective and innovative, I argued, in its use of the Vatican II documents. In my view, the documents of Vatican II provide an ampler and more authoritative view of the parish pastoral council than does the Code.

Pastoral Councils in Today's Catholic Parish was aimed in part at certain commentators who argued that canon 536 exactly represented the thinking of Vatican II. Canon 536 spoke of the "pastoral" council from the 1965 Bishops Decree, but did not use the decree's threefold description (investigate, ponder, conclude) of the pastoral council's task. For some commentators, the omission meant that the parish pastoral council did not have this threefold task. Furthermore, canon 536 did not use the verb *to coordinate* when speaking of the parish pastoral council. For some commentators, the omission meant that parish pastoral councils may not coordinate parish committees. To my mind, the commentators seemed to give greater authority to canon law than to the documents of Vatican II.[6]

The 2001 book took issue with the commentators. In particular, it argued that "coordination is within the purview" of pastoral councils.[7] To be sure, the coordination of committees is not the main work of the pastoral council. Coordination (I wrote) remains subordinate to the main work of pastoral planning, defined as the work of investigation, reflection, and the recommendation of conclusions. The book made it clear that the service of coordination should be rightly understood. It is not the "directing" of committees, but a way "to promote their success and good order as defined by their proper leaders."[8] The 2001 book tried to make room for the coordinating of parish committees as a legitimate work of the pastoral council.

On this point, my thinking has changed. The task of coordinating committees (I now concede) is *not* part of the explicit purpose of pastoral councils. When councils coordinate parish committees, they depart from their proper threefold task. Undoubtedly, the coordination of committees remains "legitimate" in the sense that it is permitted by law. Pastors may certainly ask councillors to help in this way. But properly speaking, the coordination of ministry (that is, the supervision, leadership, and governance of parish ministry) is the responsibility of the pastor. He may delegate certain tasks, but the responsibility remains his. It certainly does not belong to the pastoral council, understood as an executive or managerial body independent of him.

Since 2001 my thinking has also changed about the difference between the Bishops Decree and the Laity Decree. In 2001, I interpreted the two decrees as calling for two types of councils, the "pastoral" and the "apostolic." The pastoral council performed the threefold work of pastoral planning. The apostolic council existed to support the Church's apostolate. It could do so (I said) by coordinating lay initiatives. The key difference, I assumed, lay in the types of councils.

Today I would say that the two decrees speak of different apostolates. The "pastoral" council aids the apostolate of the pastor, the apostolate of leading the parish or diocese. The kind of council recommended in the Laity Decree should be called, not the "apostolic" council, but the "lay apostolate" council. Vatican II understood this council as supporting the largest apostolate of the Church, the apostolate of laypeople in the world. For that reason it emphasized the autonomy of the lay apostolate. The Church does not and should not attempt to govern how laypeople undertake their own work of Christian service to the world.

THE PURPOSE OF THIS BOOK

This book aims to help existing parish pastoral councils understand what they are and become more faithful to their mission. Although there are thousands of pastoral councils in the United States, not all of them interpret their task in the same way. That complicates the question of whether or not a parish council is "pastoral." Only when we clearly state what makes a council "pastoral" can we judge whether a particular council meets that standard.

Given the priest shortage, some may take issue with this book's emphasis on pastors. Critics may say, with good reason, that not all pastors are priests. Some bishops have entrusted parishes to laypeople and to deacons as parish coordinators under the supervision of a priest-moderator.[9] But the terminology of pastor remains apt. Even if the laypeople and deacons to whom bishops entrust parishes are not "pastors" in the legal sense, they function that way.[10] And the priest-pastor, in the Catholic Church, remains the norm. For those who exercise pastoral ministry but who are not priests, the thesis of this book—namely, that pastors consult councils to aid their own apostolate of parish leadership—is as relevant as it is for priest-pastors.

Others may object to this book's assumption that a single pastor leading a single parish is normal. While it may be the norm in the United States, there are many exceptions.[11] Many bishops have entrusted multiple parishes to a single pastor. This has given rise to the phenomenon of "interparochial" pastoral councils, i.e., councils made up of representatives from two or more separate parishes, all sharing the same pastor.[12] While members of these councils are drawn from different parishes, the councils remain pastoral. In other words, a single pastor consults the members who offer their services in the manner defined by the Vatican II Decree on Bishops. The assumption of a single pastor and a single parish does not change the nature of the pastoral council.

The book begins with a pretest of ten questions. The test is designed to measure the reader's pastoral council IQ. Each question has a verifiably true or false answer. The chapter explains and justifies them. At the end of chapter one, readers may have new questions about the pastoral councils that they have experienced. They may wonder whether those councils are faithful in every respect to the Church's teaching about councils as expressed in official Vatican documents.

One cannot understand pastoral councils, however, solely from the official documents. One has to have personal experience, and the first half of the book provides it. Chapters 2–7 relate a number of true stories about actual parish pastoral councils. The stories illustrate how genuinely "pastoral" councils operate. They stories explore the flavor of pastoral councils. By comparing the stories to their own experiences, readers can judge how close their own councils are to the "pastoral" ideal.

Chapters 8–13 form the second part of the book and are the most technical. These chapters lay out the Church's official teaching about councils. They relate their documentary history, i.e., how pastoral councils emerged at Vatican II and the way that pastoral councils have developed in the Church's official teaching since then. The chapters also compare the Church's ideal to a portrait of pastoral councils drawn from select guidelines published by dioceses throughout the United States. In the guidelines, we can see how diocesan officials understand the pastoral council.

There are differences, of course, between the way that Vatican documents represent the pastoral council and the way it is represented in diocesan guidelines. Parish councils in the United States are *becoming* pastoral. They are on the way. Catholics are gradually appreciating the true import of the Vatican II documents for parish pastoral councils. If this book can help diocesan officials, pastors, and parishioners understand the pastoral council better in light of its Vatican II foundations, it will have served its purpose.

NOTES

1. Vatican Council II, *Christus Dominus* (Decree Concerning the Pastoral Office of Bishops in the Church, October 28, 1965). Henceforth referred to as the Bishops Decree or Decree on Bishops.

2. Paul VI, *Encyclical of Pope Paul VI Ecclesiam Suam: The Paths of the Church* (August 6, 1964), with a Commentary by Gregory Baum, OSA (Glen Rock, NJ: Paulist Press, 1964). The third section of the encyclical is entitled "Dialogue."

3. The recommendation that the pastoral council coordinates a system of standing committees or commissions will be analyzed in Chapter 9, "Origins of the Pastoral Council."

4. Vatican Council II, *Apostolicam Actuositatem* (Decree on the Apostolate of the Laity, November 18, 1965). Henceforth referred to as the Laity Decree or Decree on the Laity.

5. Mark F. Fischer, *Pastoral Councils in Today's Catholic Parish* (Mystic, CT: Twenty-Third Publications, 2001). The book, now out 'of print, is available as a free download at http://www.mfischer.stjohnsem.edu/.

6. "It is simply false to say that the Code of Canon Law (with its silence about coordination) is superior to the documents of Vatican II or better expresses the intention of the bishops regarding parish councils." Ibid., 170. See also Mark F. Fischer, "What was Vatican II's Intent Regarding Parish Councils?" *Studia Canonica* 33 (1999): 5–25. Available at http://www.pastoralcouncils.com/.

7. Fischer, *Pastoral Councils in Today's Catholic Parish*, 171.

8. Ibid., 128.

9. John A. Renken, "The Canonical Implications of Canons 517, §2: Parishes without Resident Pastors," *Proceedings* of the Canon Law Society of America 50 (1988): 249–63; reprinted as "Parishes without a

Resident Pastor: Comments on Canon 517, §2," in *Code, Community, Ministry: Selected Studies for the Parish Minister Introducing the Code of Canon Law*, Second Revised Edition, edited by Edward G. Pfnausch (Washington, DC: Canon Law Society of America and Catholic University of America, 1992), 100–108.

10. "A parish without a resident pastor can still have a parish pastoral council, if the pastor attends its meetings as presider....Like priests, they [parish coordinators] can benefit from the study, reflection, and recommendations offered by a council. But in terms of canon law, the coordinators' councils are not 'pastoral' councils...let us call them committees, advisory groups, or boards." Fischer, *Pastoral Councils in Today's Catholic Parish*, 15–16.

11. Sixty-one percent of the dioceses that made parish changes between 1995 and 2000 created "linked" or "clustered" parishes that shared some resource, including pastors. Jeff Rexhausen et al., *A National Study of Recent Diocesan Efforts at Parish Reorganization in the United States: Pathways for the Church of the 21st Century* (Dubuque, IA: Loras College Press, 2004), iv. Rexhausen built on the work done by John P. Flaherty, ed., *Diocesan Efforts at Parish Reorganization*, report published by the Conference for Pastoral Planning and Council Development (Clearwater, FL: CPPCD, 1995).

12. Robert J. Miller, "Inter-Parochial Pastoral Councils: An Emerging Model for Parish Consultative Bodies," sponsored by the Conference for Pastoral Planning and Council Development and by the National Federation of Priests' Councils as part of the Emerging Models of Pastoral Leadership, a joint project funded by the Lilly Endowment (Archdiocese of Philadelphia: Office for Research and Planning, Director, 2007). Miller wrote that "20 percent (4,408) of the 22,203 active priests serving in parish ministry had multiple parish assignments," 1. He attributed this figure to Katarina Schuth, *Priestly Ministry in Multiple Parishes* (Collegeville, MN: Liturgical Press, 2006), 3.

CHAPTER 1

Introduction to Pastoral Councils and Pretest

In 1983, Pope John Paul II promulgated a revision of the Code of Canon Law. Canon 536 made the term *pastoral council* a part of the everyday language of parish life.[1] Prior to 1983, most people spoke of "parish" councils, not "pastoral" councils. But today, more than twenty-five years later, many people still confuse the two.

The difference is important because if we misunderstand pastoral councils, we misunderstand the intention of the Church. Pastors may expect something of pastoral councils that the Church never invited councils to offer. Councillors may not know how pastors expect them to contribute to the Church's mission. Not knowing what to expect, pastors and councillors may frustrate one another.

This book is designed to help people grasp the particular features of the pastoral council. The following pretest will help you assess your knowledge of the distinction between the "pastoral" and "parish" council. Please mark the questions true or false.

PRETEST

1. _____ . The pastoral council contributes to the apostolate of the pastor, not of the laity.

2. _____ . The main work of the pastoral council is to coordinate parish ministries.

3. _____ . *Pastoral* refers to a process apart from parliamentary procedure, to a prayerful style, and to content other than parish administration.

4. _____ . Pastors may not consult their councils about faith, orthodoxy, moral principles, or laws of the universal Church.

5. _____ . Councillors must be elected by means of a secret ballot.

6. _____ . Councils are representative in that they must reflect the demographic profile of the parish population.

7. _____ . Canon law does not require each parish to have a pastoral plan.

8. _____ . Councils guarantee the right of laypeople to bring matters to the attention of pastors.

9. _____ . Pastors consider their councillors as consultants rather than as a board of directors or governing commission.

10. _____ . On its own, the parish pastoral council never makes policy for other ministries.

THE APOSTOLATE OF PASTORS

The **first** statement, "The pastoral council contributes to the apostolate of the pastor, not of the laity," is true. *Apostolate* means "mission." The *pastoral apostolate* means "the mission of the shepherd." This is the mission of leading the parish community. Pastors fulfill their mission by preaching the gospel, celebrating the sacraments, educating parishioners, and administrating the parish's goods. They consult their people in order to make wise decisions on behalf of the parish.

Through membership on the pastoral council, parishioners participate in the apostolate of the pastor, the pastor's own office. They participate by investigating some aspect of the parish reality, reflecting on it, and recommending to him their conclusions. Parishioners often can see things that the pastor cannot see. By consulting them, he benefits from their knowledge, discernment, and insight.

Many people, however, misunderstand the pastoral council as pertaining to the lay apostolate.[2] The lay apostolate is the work of being a Christian in the world. Laypeople fulfill their apostolate when they live responsibly, contributing to society, exercising their professions faithfully, serving as good husbands and wives if married, raising their children well, honoring their parents, and caring for the poor and the sick. Leading a local congregation is not usually the duty of laypeople. That apostolate belongs normally to pastors, but laypeople contribute to it through the pastoral council.

Let us turn to the **second** statement. It affirmed that "The main work of the pastoral council is to coordinate parish ministries." This is a common opinion, but it is false. Many people view the pastoral council as the organizer of lay ministry in the parish. Strictly speaking, however, the parish priest coordinates the parish and organizes its ministries, not the council. A pastor may consult the pastoral council about how best to perform his office, but the office remains his own.

So how did people come to understand the pastoral council as the coordinator of parish activities? This book will treat that complicated question in detail. For now, however, it is enough to say that the misunderstanding is based on Vatican II's Decree on the Apostolate of Lay People.[3] The decree recommended councils at the parish level (without calling them "pastoral" councils) to promote the lay apostolate. Lay apostolate councils differ from pastoral councils, the councils in which parishioners participate in the pastor's office of shepherd. But the Vatican II recommendation of lay apostolate councils was the first reference to councils at the parish level, and the reference proved influential.

THE MATTER OF PASTORAL COUNCILS

Statement **three** is also false from the standpoint of official Church teaching. It says: "*Pastoral* refers to a process apart from parliamentary procedure, to a prayerful style, and to a content other than parish administration."

To be sure, the statement does reflect *popular* understandings of the word *pastoral*. Some people argue that such councils should not utilize parliamentary procedure, the familiar way of conducting the business of a group by motions, discussion, and voting. They object that parliamentary procedure gives an unfair advantage to those familiar with such procedure, and creates disadvantages for novices. Such critics prefer a process of discernment and consensus, believing that it is more in keeping with the council's pastoral purposes. The truth of the matter is the unscrupulous people will always take unfair advantage of those with less experience, whether they follow *Robert's Rules of Order* or an ad hoc discernment process. And the official teachings of the Church on pastoral councils do not affirm one process or another.

Another misconception about the word *pastoral* is that it describes a council that is deliberately prayerful. Instead of turning immediately to business, this type of "pastoral" council devotes a significant part of its meeting to prayer. But St. Paul advised the Thessalonians to "pray without ceasing" (1 Thess 5:17). The Church's official teachings do not say that some groups (such as "pastoral" councils) are to pray more than others. The pastoral council is pastoral because it assists the apostolate of the pastor or shepherd, not because of its discerning process and prayerful style.

A final misconception is that the word *pastoral* describes the realm of spirituality, mission, prayer, liturgy, and catechesis. In the popular imagination, pastoral councils avoid the concerns of parish business and ignore the temporal concerns of church administration. Instead, they focus on the things of God. But official Church teaching does not support this contention. Indeed, it gives pastors a great deal of latitude in consulting councils, and permits them to consult about virtually any practical matter, including administrative concerns.

This brings us to statement **four**: "Pastors may not consult their councils about faith, orthodoxy, moral principles, or laws of the universal Church." This is true. The Church distinguishes between the practical matter of parish life, about which people's opinions vary, and the truths of faith. Councils are not competent to treat dogmatic questions or matters of Christian faith. Pastors do not consult them about moral theology or canon law. But when pastors have to act in situations where the wise course depends on knowledge of the community and thorough reflection by its thoughtful members, consulting the pastoral council can prove invaluable.

COUNCILLOR SELECTION

How do pastors attract and select wise councillors? The most common procedure throughout the United States is popular election through a secret ballot. But official Church teaching does not require this practice. For that reason, statement **five**—"Councillors must be elected by means of a secret ballot"—is false. Popular election by secret ballot is normal but not required. It guarantees that the parish community has a say in who advises the pastor, but it is not the only way to choose council members.

There are numerous ways to select councillors. In some parishes, as we shall see, pastors select their councillors from among those nominated by an existing council or an ad hoc committee. In other parishes, the existing council selects replacement councillors as the terms of members end. These selection methods have the advantage of allowing knowledgeable people to discern who ought to counsel the pastor. Still other parishes try to combine the best features of popular election by secret ballot along with a process of discernment. They select councillors at an open parish meeting in which participants learn about councils, discern who might be able to serve well, and elect councillors by secret ballot from among those present.

The Church's official teaching about selecting councillors is that council members should be representative of the parish community.[4] But the official teaching has never defined what *representative* means. For some, *representative* is a demographic term. They believe that councils are representative in that their makeup mirrors the demographic profile of the parish community, with so many people of each race and an equal number of men and women, young and old. Others say that councils are representative in that the members come from each of the parish's geographic locales, or that the members represent a balance of philosophical viewpoints. No one can agree.

For that reason, statement **six** is false: "Councils are representative in that they must reflect the demographic profile of the parish population." There is no one way of being representative. And perhaps (as we shall argue) the best way of being representative is for councillors to make present the wisdom of Jesus Christ.

THE PURPOSE OF COUNCILS

The purpose of pastoral councils was first defined in Vatican II's Decree on the Pastoral Office of Bishops. There it stated that pastoral councils have a threefold purpose: they are "to investigate and consider matters relating to pastoral activity and to formulate practical conclusions concerning them."[5] This purpose, by implication, is what pastors should expect. Good councillors ought to be studying some aspect of the pastoral situation, reflecting on it, and recommending their conclusions.

In the United States, this threefold task is commonly called pastoral planning. The word *planning* expresses the responsibility of councillors. Their recommendations help pastors to arrange the parish's pastoral program systematically and to carry it out effectively.[6] The assumption, of course, is that each parish has a program, a plan to carry out the Church's work. But the Vatican has never mandated the creation of such a program or plan. Thus statement **seven** is true: "Canon law does not require each parish to have a pastoral plan." There is no such requirement in the law. Local bishops may mandate formal planning processes, but this will vary from diocese to diocese.

Many pastors say that councils are a sounding board. Councils enable them to take the pulse of the community. In the pastoral council, they say, members have a right to speak freely. The pastoral council becomes for them an instrument by which laypeople bring problems before their pastors and solve the problems by general discussion.[7] This is a common point of view, but not specific to pastoral councils. For that reason, statement **eight**—that "Councils guarantee the right of laypeople to bring matters to the attention of pastors"— is false. Canon 212 guarantees that right to all Catholics, quite apart from the pastoral council.

The purpose of the pastoral council, pastoral planning, is implicit in the Church's official description of its threefold role. Under the pastor's description, the council investigates an aspect of the pastoral situation, reflects on it, and draws appropriate conclusions. It recommends them to the pastor and, when he accepts them, they become part of the parish's pastoral plan.

COUNCILLORS AS CONSULTANTS

Acceptance of council recommendations by the pastor is important. He presides at meetings.[8] He requests the council's help. He asks its members to discharge their responsibility for studying, reflecting, and drawing conclusions in a thorough way. When their work is complete and well done, they have accomplished what the Church expects of them. These assumptions govern the work of the pastoral council. If its recommendations are well-founded and prudent, good pastors accept them.

The pastor is not obliged, however, to accept the recommendations of his councillors. The Church will not force him to accept advice he considers unwise. The Church defines the council as a *consultative* body. The pastor turns to it for rigorous study and thorough reflection, but he is not bound by its conclusions. For that reason, statement **nine** is true: "Pastors consider their councillors as consultants rather than as a board of directors or governing commission." The pastor consults his councillors because he seeks their wisdom. Their power lies not in the ability to coerce but in the prudence and excellence of their recommendations.

Some people say that the pastoral council is a leadership group. They say that the council formulates parish policy and coordinates parish committees and commissions. This statement can mislead us. To be sure, a pastor may consult his councillors when formulating policy or directing ministries. Such consultation is wise and good. But some may wrongly conclude that the council makes policy and directs ministries on its own. They mistakenly believe that the council is an independent authority. That is not the case. Councils remain consultative bodies. Statement **ten** is true: "On its own, the parish pastoral council never makes policy for other ministries." The council is not an independent authority. It does not make policy or direct ministries on its own. Pastors consult it to gain sound recommendations based on study and reflection.

THE TWO PARTS OF THIS BOOK

Having taken the pretest, you may be a little puzzled. You may be thinking that the answers do not correspond exactly to your understanding of the pastoral council. If councillors participate in the pastor's apostolate, you may ask, has the council no longer any responsibility for the lay apostolate? If the council's main work is pastoral planning, who will coordinate parish committees? And if the pastor is the one who does the consulting, do councillors no longer propose agenda items? These questions arise because the fundamental focus of the pastoral council is the apostolate of the pastor.

In order to clarify the purpose of the council, let us now see what actual pastoral councils do. Chapters 2–7 portray real councils that illuminate the pastoral ideal. The chapters not only reveal the Church's vision of pastoral councils in general, but also illustrate how actual councils are living out the ideal.

After that, the second part of the book will explore the documentary basis of the pastoral council. Chapters 8–13 will examine the Vatican documents in which the Church has described the pastoral council. The documents show how the pastoral ideal has been developed in the more than forty years since Vatican II. By that criterion, we can judge the degree to which parish councils are becoming truly pastoral.

NOTES

1. *Code of Canon Law*, Latin-English Edition, copyright 1998 by the Canon Law Society of America, reprinted in John P. Beal, James A. Coriden, and Thomas J. Green, Editors, *New Commentary on the Code of Canon Law*, commissioned by the Canon Law Society of America (New York and Mahwah, NJ: Paulist Press, 2000). See canon 536.

2. The viewpoint that the pastoral council is meant to promote the lay apostolate of Christian service to the world will be explored in chapter 9, "Origins of the Pastoral Council."

3. Councils to assist the Church's apostolic work "can take care of the mutual coordinating of the various lay associations and undertakings, the autonomy and particular nature of each remaining untouched." Vatican Council II, *Apostolicam actuositatem* (Decree on the Apostolate of Lay People, November 18, 1965), no. 26, translated by Father Finnian, OCSO, in *Vatican Council II*, ed. Austin Flannery, vol. 1: *The Conciliar and Post Conciliar Documents* (Northport, NY: Costello Publishing Company, 1998), 791.

4. "As far as the composition of the pastoral council is concerned, although the members of the council cannot in a juridical sense be called representatives of the total diocesan community, nevertheless, as far as possible, they should present a witness or sign of the entire diocese, and, therefore, it seems extremely opportune that priests, religious and laity who expound various requirements and experiences take part in the council." Sacred Congregation for the Clergy, *Omnes Christifideles* (Circular Letter on "Pastoral Councils," January 25, 1973), no. 7, reprinted in James I. O'Connor,

ed., "Officially Published Documents Affecting the Code of Canon Law 1973–1977," *Canon Law Digest* 8: (1978): 280–288. The circular letter was also published in *Origins* 3:12 (9/15/73): 186–190. The text is available online at www.pastoralcouncils.com/bibliography/vatican-documents/post conciliar/circular/.

5. "It will be the function of this [pastoral] council to investigate and consider matters relating to pastoral activity and to formulate practical conclusions concerning them." Vatican Council II, *Christus Dominus* (Decree on the Pastoral Office of Bishops in the Church, October 28, 1965), no. 27, translated by Matthew Dillon, OSB, Edward O'Leary, OP, and "AF" [Austin Flannery] in *Vatican Council II*, ed. Austin Flannery, vol. 1: *The Conciliar and Post Conciliar Documents* (Northport, NY: Costello Publishing Company, 1998), 580.

6. "The pastoral council, in which specially chosen clergy, religious and laity have part…by its study and consideration should provide the necessary conclusions so that the diocesan community may be able to arrange its pastoral program systematically and carry it out effectively." Sacred Congregation for Bishops, *De Sacerdotio ministeriali* (The Ministerial Priesthood, November 30, 1971), published in reference to canon 329 in "Officially Published Documents Affecting the Code of Canon Law 1968–1972," ed. James I. O'Connor, *Canon Law Digest* 7 (1975): 342–366. See part 2, §3, "Relations between priests and lay persons," 364. This teaching was reaffirmed by the Sacred Congregation for the Bishops in its 2004 "Directory for the Pastoral Ministry of Bishops" (*Apostolorum successores*, no. 184), which will be discussed in chapter 13.

7. Vatican Council II, *Apostolicam actuositatem* (Decree on the Apostolate of Lay People), no. 10: "The laity should develop the habit of working in the parish in close union with their priests, of bringing before the ecclesial community their own problems, world problems, and questions regarding man's salvation, to examine them together and solve them by general discussion."

8. "It is for the Parish Priest to preside at parochial councils" (*Ecclesiae de Mysterio* [Instruction on Certain Questions Regarding Collaboration of the Non-Ordained Faithful in the Sacred Ministry of Priest]), §3 Early parish council publications, however, would typically speak of the elected lay leader of the council (not the pastor) as the "president." See Robert C. Broderick, *The Parish Council Handbook: A Handbook to Bring the Power of Renewal to Your Parish* (Chicago: Franciscan Herald Press, 1968), 45; Bernard Lyons, *Parish Councils: Renewing the Christian Community* (Techny, IL: Divine Word Publications, 1967), 135; and Edward E. Ryan, *How to Establish a Parish Council: A Step-by-Step Program for Setting Up Parish Councils* (Chicago: Claretian, 1968), 27.

CHAPTER 2

What Councils Do

The following sketch of an actual pastoral council answers the question of what councils do. Of course, it is difficult to give a general answer. Parish priests may consult their pastoral councils about virtually any practical matter. But regarding the pastor, this much can be said with confidence. When he consults, he is asking the pastoral council to do three things:

1) Study a particular matter

2) Reflect about it

3) Recommend its conclusions.

Similarly, we can confidently describe the pastoral councillors' role. They agree to undertake a threefold responsibility. They inquire about some aspect of the parish reality, weigh the importance of what they have learned, and recommend their findings to the pastor. He consults. They investigate, consider, and report to him. In order to illustrate this relationship, consider the following example.

In 1940, St. Mary Magdalen Church was founded in Camarillo, fifty miles from Los Angeles. The parish's original chapel was built in 1914 by the family of Adolfo Camarillo whose father lent his name to the city. St. Mary Magdalen Chapel still stands upon a hill, twelve miles inland from the Pacific Ocean, and once overlooked hundreds of acres of orchards, especially lemons and oranges. In the summer, the scent of the citrus blossoms would fill the air. At one time many parishioners were Spanish-speaking farmworkers but, in recent years, the city of Camarillo has become a large suburban center. It includes numerous retirees and many others who commute to Los Angeles and Santa Barbara on the Ventura Freeway. Camarillo has grown to such an extent that St. Mary Magdalen parish built a large new church in the western part of the city.

ST. MARY'S FIRST COUNCIL

When Father James Stehly became the pastor of St. Mary Magdalen in 1999, it was his first pastorate. He himself had grown up on his family's farm not far from Camarillo, and he was raised with a sympathetic appreciation for the hard life of farmworkers. Within his initial three years at St. Mary Magdalen he created a parish pastoral council. It too was a first in the parish's history, since Father Stehly's predecessor had never established one. The new pastoral council had twenty-two members, chosen by Father Stehly to represent different facets of the parish, such as the Knights of Columbus, the parish school, the Spanish-speaking leadership group, the parish's small church communities, the charismatic prayer group, Our Lady's Blue Army, the older adult services and intervention system, the respect life ministry, the Vietnamese community, and the parish's young adults. I remember attending one of the first meetings of the council, its members seated in an enormous circle in the parish hall.

The council, however, was not markedly successful. The members had been told that they were representatives of the community, but they were unsure about how to represent their constituencies. Some viewed themselves as advocates for their portion of the parish community, seeking a larger share of the parish's resources and the pastor's time. Others saw themselves as representatives at large. They pursued diverse agendas, trying to persuade the pastor to buy more property, or to expand the parochial school, or to construct a lighted sign advertising the parish. Father Stehly had hoped that the pastoral council would enable him to communicate more effectively with his large parish and coordinate its activities. "I had hoped to share responsibility for the parish with council members," he mused, "but much of every meeting was devoted to reports by this group or that, and people just got tired of it." Attendance dropped. Although the council never disbanded, by 2003 it had shrunk by almost two-thirds.

That year, 2003, was remarkable in the history of the Archdiocese of Los Angeles. In May, a two-year-long consultation culminated in a synod, a gathering of hundreds of delegates from each parish, including St. Mary Magdalen. The synod sessions were held at the pastoral center of the newly-built Cathedral of Our Lady of the Angels in downtown Los Angeles. The cathedral is a modern structure overlooking the city's traditional pueblo and plaza. Synod delegates identified six areas of pastoral concern and recommended that Cardinal Roger Mahony consider them as priorities. The six areas were:

Evangelization
Church structures for participation and accountability
Christian education and formation
Lay and ordained leadership
Eucharist and sacramental life
Social justice.[1]

Father Stehly and several of his pastoral councillors attended the synod sessions. They were happy when Cardinal Mahony formally accepted the synod recommendations on September 4, 2003. He invited the archdiocese to begin considering how to implement them at the parish level.

THE RELEVANCE OF SOCIAL JUSTICE

The synod sessions impressed Father Stehly as purposeful and practical. He noted that the cardinal himself was directing the synod, consulting the people of the archdiocese, asking them to help him define its priorities for the new millennium. The cardinal had a definite end in mind, the prioritizing of pastoral initiatives, and was asking his people to nominate the areas in which the archdiocesan Church should concentrate its energy and resources. While the synod participants were clearly "representative"—they were chosen to represent the 287 parishes of the archdiocese—they were not lobbying for advantages or advocating for their constituencies. They were engaged in a group process designed to distil their wisdom and express it in the form of practical recommendations. This kind of "representation" seemed clearer than the representation that had proven so difficult at St. Mary Magdalen.

Father Stehly also admired the results of the synod. He felt that the six pastoral priorities adroitly expressed the needs of the archdiocesan Church. He was especially interested in the sixth pastoral priority about social justice. Under that heading fell five "pastoral strategies," designed by the synod for mobilizing social justice efforts. The fourth strategy especially caught Father Stehly's eye. It stated, "Parishes are to establish an outreach ministry that cares for parishioners and others with particular needs by caring for them directly or referring them to appropriate social services."[2] Father Stehly had always felt that efforts on behalf of social justice are essential features of parish life. St. Mary Magdalen Parish did not have a social justice committee. Father Stehly felt that this was a deficit, and he began to consider how to establish one.

Father Stehly knew that questions about social justice are delicate. Early in his pastorate he had made some liturgical changes, changes that some parishioners felt were unjust, and parishioners complained about them. In Father Stehly's eyes, the changes had been minor. He had moved the U.S. flag off the main altar, introduced a number of new hymns, and directed the altar servers to sit in the front pew during the Liturgy of the Word. Some parishioners, however, were upset by these changes. On one occasion, a few of them had asked to speak to Father Stehly after the Sunday evening mass. When mass was over, some fifty people, recruited by the initial few, remained in the church to express their grievances.

The "unjust" changes offended parishioners for various reasons. Some felt that the absence of the flag was unpatriotic. Others complained the movement of the altar servers to the pews during the Liturgy of the Word signaled a departure from hallowed tradition. (These were mainly the parents of the servers, who liked to see their children on the altar.) But the most vociferous complaints were about the new hymns. Some people found them difficult to sing, and still others disliked the "new theology" they represented. They said that the hymns overemphasized the People of God and de-emphasized the real presence of Christ in the Eucharist. Many viewed the hymns as "supplanting" the cherished older hymns of the parish. One person angrily said, "If these changes continue, Father, we may have to drive to the St. Bonaventure Mission where they still celebrate the

Latin Mass." The complaining parishioners had strong feelings, and Father Stehly did not want to alienate them further.

At the same time, however, the priest did not want those strong feelings to paralyze the parish. He was still interested in creating a social justice committee. But he realized that he would have to be very prudent in making further changes. He needed to anticipate their consequences and ready the congregation before implementing them.

THE SECOND COUNCIL'S ASSIGNMENT

So Father Stehly turned to the parish's pastoral council, which by this time had shrunk from the initial twenty-two members to a mere eight. At the November 16, 2004, meeting, he reviewed the synod initiative about social justice with the councillors. He observed that there was no social justice committee at the parish. He then asked the members present, "How should we respond as a parish to the synod initiative? Do we need to establish a social justice committee?"

Carlos Tamayo, a dentist and a representative of the parish's Spanish-speaking community, had reviewed the agenda and prepared a response. At the meeting he distributed a one-page handout that listed thirty-nine different parish initiatives and ministerial groups. It showed that some parishioners were engaged already in social justice through traditional Catholic organizations, such as Catholic Charities and the Knights of Columbus. Others, such as the members of the *Sociedad Guadalupana* and the parish's health ministry, were engaged in direction action on behalf of the needy. Still other groups, like BASIC (Brothers and Sisters in Christ), were committed to the formation of young people. Tamayo summed up his point of view in a question: "Aren't all of these groups already doing social justice?"

Cecilia Kwolek, a parishioner who participated in several parish organizations, agreed. "I belong to a group that feeds the poor," she said. "Isn't that what the synod means by peace and justice?" Robert Riddle, the chairperson of the pastoral council, also expressed some doubts. "We know that parishioners are engaged in many social justice activities," he observed. "But we do not know very much about the activities, such as how many people participate in them and how many people they serve." Riddle said that the council needed to learn more about the existing parish ministries.

His suggestion persuaded Father Stehly. By the end of that November meeting, the councillors had reviewed the list of thirty-nine ministerial groups on Carlos Tamayo's list. With Father Stehly's encouragement, they identified twenty-one groups whose parish work included at least some activities on behalf of social justice. Bob Riddle, the chairman, came up with four questions for each group:

> What does the organization do to promote social justice?
> How does it promote justice? What resources does it use?
> What have been the organization's most important
>   achievements?

Councillors volunteered to contact two, three, or more groups, note their answers, and present them at subsequent pastoral council meetings.

The work that Father Stehly and Bob Riddle had invited the councillors to undertake was a good example of appreciative inquiry.[3] Appreciative inquiry is an investigative approach that starts with a distinct presupposition. Instead of assuming that that a community or organization is a problem to be solved, it assumes that it has its own life and accomplishments. Inquiry about the community does not begin by focusing on dysfunction, but on its identity as gifted individuals with a common cause. Commencing with esteem for the community's identity and mission, appreciative inquiry discovers successes and solves problems within a positive context. By asking the pastoral council to study how the various parish organizations contribute to social justice, the pastor and the chairman were showing respect for the accomplishments of parishioners.

THE COUNCIL'S FINDINGS

Throughout the winter months, the pastoral council made inquiries among the various parish groups. At the March 15, 2005, meeting, the council reviewed its findings. The members had contacted seventeen different parish organizations and asked them the questions proposed by Bob Riddle. They discovered that a number of parish organizations already provided direct care to needy people. The sewing circle, for example, prepares layettes for newborn infants.

The Family to Family ministry serves a free breakfast one Sunday a month. The respect life ministry counsels unmarried pregnant women. In addition, several organizations offered indirect support and referral. The Knights of Columbus contribute to the county's efforts to help the homeless. The health ministry promotes parish and community services to those facing medical crises. Parishioners staff an office of Catholic Charities that helps older adults remain independent. After digesting this information, some members of the pastoral council expressed surprise that St. Mary Magdalen did so much for social justice. There was no need to establish a new parish office, the council concluded. Social justice at the parish was not being neglected. On the contrary, parishioners showed deep engagement. The council's findings had proven genuinely appreciative.

The work of the pastoral council helped Father Stehly realize that the establishment of a new parish office of social justice might be taken as a slight to the many organizations already contributing to justice in their own ways. "When I had first considered the social justice ministry," Father Stehly said, "I was not thinking primarily of the sewing circle, the health ministry, and the Knights of Columbus." But by asking the council to inquire about what parishioners were already doing on behalf of justice, he gained a renewed appreciation of their efforts. They might not have been doing justice in the way he had first imagined, but they were indeed providing the direct and indirect services mentioned in the archdiocesan synod initiative. He wanted to honor their efforts.

As a consequence of the council's deliberations, Father Stehly responded in two ways. The first had to do with the parish Web site. He asked the Web master to add "Ministries and Organizations" link to the parish's splash page. The new link described the various organizations, highlighting their contributions precisely as contributions to social justice. Father Stehly's second response concerned education and formation. The work of the pastoral council had showed him that St. Mary Magdalen parishioners were deeply committed to social justice. But some parish service providers did not understand their efforts as a participation in the Church's social teaching. Moreover, they were often unaware of other justice efforts taking place within the parish but outside their own group. Father Stehly asked one of the parish's permanent deacons to develop a plan to gather the groups as a whole for prayer and occasionally to hear a speaker. The pastor felt that this would honor their ministries, support them, and raise their awareness of the Church's worldwide mission.

WHAT THE COUNCIL DID

The work of the St. Mary Magdalen pastoral council on the social justice initiative was by no means the most important thing that the council did during my brief acquaintance with the members. But the work illustrates well the formal relationship between pastor and councillors implicit in the Church's official documents.[4] Father Stehly approached the council with a question. He wanted to know how St. Mary's should respond to the archdiocesan synod's social justice initiative and whether the parish should establish a social justice committee. By asking these questions, Father Stehly was not abdicating his responsibility for the parish. On the contrary, he was seeking the wisdom of parishioners so that he could make a sound decision.

The council members, for their part, responded to Father Stehly's request and exercised their responsibility thoroughly. They contacted parish organizations. They posed important questions. They gathered and synthesized the answers. They weighed the consequences. In the end, they recommended that the pastor not establish a new parish office, but instead support existing ministries through prayer and education. When Father Stehly accepted their recommendations, the council's work was complete. The council had helped him to understand the parish better, to avoid innovations that might have damaged parish morale, and to support the work of the parish community.

Working on social justice with the smaller council had clarified Father Stehly's thinking about the representative nature of the pastoral council. Recall that his initial council was composed of twenty-two members. They were chosen to represent the many organizations and facets of the parish. But the word *representative* was ambiguous. Some councillors felt that they were to advocate the interests of their constituencies. Others believed that they were to influence the pastor by swaying him with their best thinking about the parish. American Catholics understand "representation" in a variety of ways, not all of which pastors find helpful.

After the archdiocesan synod, Father Stehly firmly directed the council toward the social justice initiative. He invited them to help him consider how the parish could respond to it. And when the councillors contacted the various parish organization, inquiring about what they do and whom they serve, the councillors were being representative in a particular way. Although they may not have been representing a particular constituency, they "represented" by "making present" the wisdom of the community. Councillors are not legal representatives of the parish. They can be a sign, however, of the parish's common sense. When Father Stehly accepted the council's recommendations, he implicitly acknowledged the wisdom "made present" in them.

Parish pastoral councils do not exist to represent the voice of laypeople or guarantee their right to be heard. They are not meant to be an expression of the lay apostolate. Every Catholic already has a right to bring his or her concerns to the pastor's attention. Pastoral councils exist rather as a participation in the apostolate of the pastor. The members share in the pastor's mission or office of leading the parish. When the St. Mary Magdalen pastoral council reflected on the parish's social justice activities and presented their conclusions to Father Stehly, they shared in his apostolate. They helped him make a wise decision. That is what pastoral councils are supposed to do.

NOTES

1. Cardinal Roger Mahony and the People of God of the Archdiocese of Los Angeles, *Gathered and Sent: Documents of the Synod of the Archdiocese of Los Angeles 2003*, bilingual (English/Spanish) edition, edited by Kris Fankhouser et al. (Chicago: Liturgy Training Publications, 2003).

2. Ibid., 80.

3. For an application of appreciative inquiry to pastoral planning see Susan Star Paddock, *Appreciative Inquiry in the Catholic Church* (Plano, TX: Thin Book Publishing, 2003). Appreciative inquiry was first treated by David L. Cooperrider, Suresh Srivastva, and associates, *Appreciative Management and Leadership* (San Francisco: Jossey-Bass, 1990). Other writers have applied the principles of appreciative leadership in David L. Cooperrider, Peter F. Sorensen, Jr., Diana Whitney, and Therese F. Yaeger, Editors, *Appreciative Inquiry: Rethinking the Organization Toward a Positive Theory of Change* (Champaign, IL: Stipes Publishing, 2000).

The application of appreciative leadership to parish councils was treated in Mark F. Fischer, "Breathe Fresh Spirit into Your Parish Pastoral Council," *Today's Parish* (January 1997): 29–31. The most recent application is by David DeLambo and Richard Krivanka, "Appreciative Inquiry: A Powerful Process for Parish Listening and Planning," chap. 5 in Mark F. Fischer and Mary Margaret Raley, Editors, *Four Ways to Build More Effective Parish Councils: A Pastoral Approach* (Mystic, CT: Twenty-Third Publications, 2002), 87–101.

4. Vatican Council II, *Christus Dominus* (Decree on the Pastoral Office of Bishops in the Church), no. 27, is the basic source for the three-fold role of the pastoral council: investigating, pondering, and reaching conclusions.s

CHAPTER 3

Councils and Committees

A pastoral council is a planning body. Under the pastor's direction it studies and considers some aspect of the pastoral situation, and recommends its conclusions to the pastor. When he accepts the council's recommendations and puts them into practice, the work of the council is complete. Strictly speaking, the council plans but does not implement.

Many U.S. councils mistakenly view themselves, however, as bodies that implement as well as plan. The pastoral council, they say, is a "council of ministries."[1] It implements policies through a system of ministerial committees or commissions. In a later chapter we will examine the source of this misconception and how widespread it is. For the present, it is enough to say that Vatican's official documents on pastoral councils do not mention standing committees or commissions.[2] Nor do they give pastoral councils the authority to coordinate.[3] Moreover, popular authors have also questioned the idea that pastoral councils coordinate committees.[4] The task of the pastoral council, we can therefore say, is pastoral planning, but not supervising the implementation of plans.

In order to understand the proper planning role of pastoral councils and committees, consider the following story. It is about a parish committee—in this case, not even a committee of the pastoral council. The committee developed a proposal for an outreach to Africa.

GENESIS OF THE AFRICA COMMITTEE

St. Julie Billiart Church in Newbury Park, California, is named for the nineteenth-century co-foundress of the Sisters of Notre Dame de Namur. St. Julie formed the community of religious women, shortly after the French Revolution. She was elevated to sainthood in 1969. The California parish named for her was opened that same year.

The pastor of St. Julie Billiart Church is Msgr. Michael Bunny, "Father Mike" to his parishioners. He was ordained in 1965 and has been pastor of St. Julie since 1997. Although the parish lacks a parochial school, it has a flourishing youth ministry and confirmation preparation program. Each year, during spring vacation, more than 140 parish young people spend a week in Tijuana, Mexico, about 220 miles away. Under the watchful eye of adult supervisors, the youth construct simple one-room homes for Tijuana's poor. In 2008, the young people built nine homes. Father Mike is justifiably proud of the confirmation program. It raises the consciousness of young people and offers a tangible benefit to the people of Tijuana.

The Mexico mission trip was the brainchild of Dave Smith, a retired police officer and newly-ordained permanent deacon who is Director of Faith Formation at St. Julie's. Smith has been coordinating the Mexico trip for more than eight years, ever since his youngest son was in the confirmation program. The mission trip now involves some thirty adults and has a budget of more than $70,000, which covers the cost of transportation, construction materials, and food. Funding for the trip comes from freewill offerings at the parish and the money raised by the young people. Smith jokes that he will continue the annual Mexico trip until he can no longer wield a hammer.

But Smith's concern for the poor does not stop with the people of Tijuana. He has a vision for social outreach and stewardship at St. Julie Church. "We should not just be concerned with the needy in our own back yards," he said, "but also with the poorest of the poor." For some years, Smith has been thinking about African missions. He knew that a nearby evangelical church had pledged a portion of its capital campaign to a project in Africa. Smith felt that St. Julie ought to do the same. In 2006, Smith made a proposal to Father Mike. He proposed that the parish initiate a form of material support and outreach to Africa's poor.

Father Mike had a lot of respect for Dave Smith. He recognized that Smith's proposal was broad in scope and would have many consequences. What kind of aid would the parish offer? Who in Africa would the Church serve? Would the parish support such a mission? The proposal was very general and did not answer these questions in

detail. Father Mike brought up the proposal at a meeting of his pastoral council. Broad questions are appropriate for such a council, and
questions about the African mission fit the council's threefold portfolio of study, reflection, and discernment. But the pastoral council
was already busy with other endeavors. So Father Mike asked Dave
Smith, in his role as Director of Faith Formation, to form a committee. The committee's task was to explore the rationale for the
African mission, consider what types of outreach the parish could
support, and recommend a concrete plan by 2008.

THE COMMITTEE'S FIRST MEETING

The first meeting of the St. Julie's African Aid Committee
(SJAAC) took place on December 6, 2006, with eleven attendees.
Dave Smith chaired the committee, beginning with a prayer and
inviting the members to share their reflections on the task and their
motives for participating. The members included a homemaker, a
professor, an accountant, a high school teacher, and two couples.
One of the couples, Jim and Connie Olson, had had a lot of travel
experience. Jim Olson had retired from a career with the Los Angeles
Museum of Natural History, and had visited Africa on numerous
occasions. In his work he had had firsthand experience of the diffi-
culties of travel and communication in Africa.

Three topics emerged on December 6 that the St. Julie's
African Aid Committee would return to again and again. The first
was the most general, and it was Dave Smith himself who raised it.
"Why should St. Julie Church support a mission in Africa," he asked,
"when there are so many needy people in our own country?" The
SJAAC members were already interested in the mission, he said, or
they wouldn't have come to the meeting. But the rest of the parish
will want an answer. The amount the parish will want to contribute,
he said, depends upon the persuasiveness of the answer. .

The second topic was related to the first, and again it was Smith
who brought it up. Let us suppose, he said, that the parish decides to
establish an outreach to Africa. What kind of outreach should it be?
In reply, the SJAAC members agreed that St. Julie Church should
contribute to an existing African project, such as Catholic Relief
Services, or other private initiatives, or an existing parish or diocese

in Africa. Sue Reyes, a high school teacher, noted that the Sisters of Notre Dame have a mission in Africa. Reyes taught at the sisters' La Reina High School, about five miles from St. Julie Church. The members agreed that the parish could even support a mission like that of the sisters.

The third topic was about stewardship, or rather, about the criteria for deciding what African mission should receive the parish's support. One member of the committee, a homemaker named Sue Pertessis, said that the aid should go to needy Africans, not to the administrators of aid projects. Another committee member, an accountant named Steve Ferrari, made a similar suggestion. He said that the parish should try not just to alleviate the symptoms of poverty, but to get at the root of problems that create poverty. By the end of the December 6 meeting, the members had begun to realize how complicated the development of an African mission could be.

WHAT THE COMMITTEE DID

After the first meeting in 2006, the St. Julie's African Aid Committee met an additional seven times in 2007. During those meetings, the SJAAC considered a number of organizations to which the parish might contribute, like Heifer International. Established in 1944 and now based in Little Rock, Arkansas, Heifer International has enabled some seven million needy families to acquire livestock. It helps train them to care for the animals and teaches them how to put them to good use. Committee member Connie Olson described how she and her husband, Jim, had purchased a goat for a young boy. She sketched the basic principles of the Heifer organization, including accountability, sustainability, and justice.

The committee also heard a presentation from a student at St. John's Seminary, which belongs to the Archdiocese of Los Angeles. The student, born in the Congolese Diocese of Tshumbe, had received a scholarship from the archdiocese. Albert Shuyaka showed slides of the Congo and narrated what it was like to grow up in the Kasaï Oriental district. He described the agricultural lifestyle of his family, the risk to crops from monkeys, the commonplace experience of malaria, and the high incidence of infant mortality. He even told the story of his 185-kilometer walk each fall from his village to the

Catholic seminary in Lodja, and the time he was robbed by rebel soldiers. The initial meetings of the committee enriched the members' knowledge of Africa and made them more realistic about what St. Julie Billiart Church could do.

The committee's May 2 meeting was a turning point. Reflecting on their progress, the members made a number of decisions. First of all, they agreed that they wanted to support a Catholic organization, rather than one that was nondenominational. Further, they wanted to support an effort with whose representatives in Africa they could have a permanent and personal connection. For the committee members, those decisions seemed to rule out Heifer International.

In addition, the members agreed on May 2 that they wanted to lend their support to a part of Africa that was politically stable and in which English was a major language. If the parish were to have a mission in Africa, parishioners wanted to be able to communicate easily and to send materials or cash safely. That took the Congo off the parish's list. In the Congo, French is the major European language, and the country has been embroiled in a civil war for many years.

The committee's most important decision, however, was about supporting or "adopting" a parish. Members had established contacts with a pastor in Zambia and in Uganda, and the two parishes were potential adoptees. Jim Olson offered to draft a proposal, which was discussed at the May 16 meeting. After reviewing the first draft, members said that they wanted to clarify what "adoption" meant, that is, to state the extent of St. Julie's legal responsibility for any parish that it might adopt. They also said that the proposal should spell out how the African parish would be accountable to St. Julie's, and how St. Julie's parish would establish an advisory board to monitor its relation to the African parish. By the end of the May 16 meeting, the members felt that they were almost ready to report their findings to Father Mike. Jim Olson went to work on draft two of the proposal.

AN UNEXPECTED SHIFT

At the August 9 meeting, the committee discussed Jim Olson's second draft. The introduction to the draft said that St. Julie's will adopt an African parish, but it also said that St. Julie's will work with "communities." A committee member asked for a clarification. Does St. Julie's hope to adopt one parish or multiple communities? In reply, Olson said that it was too early to tell. He was organizing a fact-finding trip in February of 2008. The trip would cost each participant about $3000, he said, and members who wanted to go would have to fund their own travel expenses. There was no way to really reach a decision, Olson argued, without an actual site visit.

Dave Smith was also enthusiastic about the trip. Smith said that he and Olson hoped to not just visit parishes in Zambia and Uganda, but also to visit a school in Uganda run by the Notre Dame Sisters. The other committee members asked for more information about the school. Olson said that he would try to arrange a meeting between the committee members and Notre Dame Sister Kristin Battles. Sister Kristin was the sisters' local superior, and had just returned from a trip to Uganda.

On September 4, the SJAAC met Sr. Kristin at the convent of the Sisters of Notre Dame in Thousand Oaks. She told the members that the sisters had built two schools in Uganda. In 1998 they established the coeducational St. Julie Primary School and in 2003 the all-girls Notre Dame Academy Senior Secondary School. The two boarding schools are staffed by ten sisters and thirty Ugandans, said Sr. Kristin. Ugandan construction firms, established by the White Fathers and employing hundreds of local workers, built the thirty structures in Buseesa at a cost of more than two million dollars. The California and Kentucky provinces of the Sisters of Notre Dame contribute about $100,000 annually to the Buseesa mission, Sr. Kristin added. This year the first class of seniors will graduate from the academy, she said, and all are going on to higher education.

Sister Kristin's presentation greatly impressed the committee members. The Buseesa mission, they felt, was just what the committee had been looking for. It was a Catholic initiative, and through the sisters St. Julie Church would have a direct connection to the mission. The language of instruction in Uganda is English, and the country enjoys relative stability. Moreover, the Buseesa mission had one great advantage that the adopt-a-parish proposal did not have. Several committee members had voiced the fear that, if St. Julie's were to establish a relationship with an African parish, and if later the African pastor were transferred by his bishop, a breakdown in communication might result. Supporting the sisters' schools in Uganda (rather than a parish) would ensure constant communication, with no danger from a change in African personnel. By the end of the September 4 meeting, the members generally agreed that support for the Buseesa mission was preferable to adopting a parish.

FATHER MIKE'S RESPONSE

In February 2008, Dave Smith, Jim Olson, and a few other parishioners made a two-week trip to Africa. They visited the Notre Dame Sisters' two schools in Buseesa, and came back with great respect for them. The visitors to Africa met one more time with the other members of the committee. They showed photos and related their experiences. The consensus was that St. Julie's should adopt, not a parish, but the two Buseesa schools. That was the committee's last meeting.

Let us consider, for a moment, the relationship between the St. Julie's African Aid Committee and the parish pastoral council. When Dave Smith first brought the idea for an African mission to Father Mike, the pastor wanted more consultation, but the parish pastoral council was busy with other matters. Father Mike asked Smith to establish the SJAAC. The committee was an ad hoc committee, not a standing committee, because it was to finish its work by 2008. Further, the SJAAC was not a committee of the pastoral council, but rather was a committee of the parish. The pastoral council did not supervise the work of the committee; Dave Smith, the Director of Faith Formation, supervised it.

The purpose of the committee was not, strictly speaking, to create an African mission. Neither the committee nor Dave Smith had a legal right to make decisions on behalf of the parish. They did not "represent" it in a legal sense. They could not establish a parish mission independently of the pastor. No, the committee's purpose was to explore the rationale for the mission, to consider different types of mission, and to recommend a concrete plan. The committee members successfully completed their work by February 2008.

Having received the report from St. Julie's African Aid Committee, Father Mike now had a decision to make. He could accept the committee's proposal outright and allocate a portion of the parish budget to the mission. Or he could ask the committee to do further research. He took the second approach. He asked the committee to be more specific about its goal. The members, after a discussion with Sr. Kristin Battles, recommended that the parish ask for contributions toward the $50,000 price of a new dormitory for the St. Julie Primary School in Buseesa. On the weekend of January 23 to 24, 2010, the parish sponsored a special collection and raised $7,293 toward that goal.

Thanks to the work of the SJAAC, Father Mke was no longer considering a vague dream of support for Africa in general. No, he accepted the specific recommendation to support a school in Buseesa run by the Notre Dame Sisters, who have a convent near the parish, a religious order founded by the parish's own patron saint.

PASTORAL COUNCILS AND PARISH COMMITTEES

The pastoral council and committees such as St. Julie's African Aid Committee have a specific planning function. They investigate, reflect, and recommend conclusions to the pastor (or, in the case of the SJAAC, to a member of his staff). Council and committee serve the pastoral apostolate, in that they help Father Mike to make decisions on the parish's behalf. He consults them in order to make wise choices.

It is common throughout the United States, however, for pastoral councils to view themselves as having more than a consultative role. In a later chapter we will see that many guidelines for councils published by U.S. dioceses describe the pastoral council as the coordinator of a system of committees or commissions.[5] Some councils believe that they coordinate committees by developing policy, policy that the committees are meant to implement. For the implementation of these policies, some authors even say, pastoral councils should hold committees accountable.[6]

The Vatican's official documents do not endorse this view of the pastoral council as the coordinator of a system of committees. They do not call for a system of standing committees and they do not give the council executive authority. To be sure, some pastors may ask councils to coordinate committees in order to promote good communication with them. Many diocesan documents reflect this practice.[7] But when councillors coordinate, they do so as volunteers under the pastor's direction. He directs parish ministries through committees and commissions. There is an extensive literature about how pastors can utilize such parish structures.[8]

The coordination of committees, however, is not a formal feature of the "pastoral" council. It does not assign to pastoral councils the work of coordination. Indeed, it is hared to imagine how a pastoral council—by definition, a group of volunteers that usually meets once a month—could coordinate all parish ministries. Directing parish organizations is ultimately the responsibility of the pastor and the parish staff under his leadership.

That was certainly true at St. Julie Billiart parish. Father Mike normally asks the parish pastoral council to study, discern, and reach conclusions. He does not ask it to coordinate a system of parish standing committees, or even to coordinate an ad hoc committee like the African mission. He entrusted that role to Dave Smith. Thanks to him and his committee, St. Julie Billiart Church in California has made a substantial contribution to the wellbeing of another institution with the same patron: St. Julie Billiart Primary School and the Senior Secondary School, run by the Sisters of Notre Dame de Namur in Buseesa, Uganda.

NOTES

1. To my knowledge, Thomas Sweetser and Carol Wisniewski Holden were the first to use the term "council of ministries" in *Leadership in a Successful Parish* (San Francisco: Harper & Row, 1987), 126. William J. Rademacher with Marliss Rogers also recommended a system of standing committees in *The New Practical Guide for Parish Councils* (Mystic, CT: Twenty-Third Publications, 1988), 115 ff.

2. Vatican II's *Christus Dominus* (Decree on Bishops), the fundamental document on pastoral councils, stated at no. 27 that they have a threefold function (investigating, pondering, and reaching conclusions). It does not mention committees, commissions, or lay initiatives. Virtually identical language describes pastoral councils in Pope Paul VI's Apostolic Letter *Ecclesiae Sanctae I* at no. 16; in the 1971 document of the Synod of Bishops entitled *De Sacerdotio ministeriali* (The Ministerial Priesthood), part 2, §3, p. 364; in the 1973 *Ecclesiae imago* (Directory on the Pastoral Ministry of Bishops) by the Sacred Congregation for Bishops, no. 204, p. 105; in the 1973 *Omnes*

Christifideles (Circular Letter on "Pastoral Councils") by the Sacred Congregation for Clergy, no. 9; and in c. 511 of the 1983 *Code of Canon Law*. To be sure, these documents refer mainly to pastoral councils at the diocesan level. The 1973 Circular Letter (the only Vatican document devoted in its entirety to pastoral councils) explicitly extended the language about Diocesan Pastoral Councils to Parish Pastoral Councils.

In 2002 an Instruction by the Vatican's Congregation for the Clergy, entitled *The Priest, Pastor and Leader of the Parish Community* (no. 26), reaffirmed the connection between diocesan pastoral councils and parish pastoral councils. The same connection was also reaffirmed by the Congregation for Bishops in the 2004 *Apostolorum successores* (Directory for the Pastoral Ministry of Bishops), no. 184. In my view, this evidence is decisive. The consistent threefold description of the "pastoral" council in Vatican documents, and the application of this to parish councils in the two documents of the Congregation for the Clergy, suggest that *parish* pastoral councils foster pastoral activity in the same threefold way as do pastoral councils in general. This argument will be laid out in detail below in chaps. 8–13.

3. See *Ad gentes divinitus* (Decree on the Church's Missionary Activity, December 7, 1965), trans. by Redmond Fitzmaurice, in *Vatican Council II*, ed. Austin Flannery, vol. 1: *The Conciliar and Post-Conciliar Documents*, 673–704. The decree states that Diocesan Pastoral Councils may coordinate lay apostolates (no. 30, 847). This comment may lead some to conclude that *parish* pastoral councils have a coordinating function. The Missionary Decree pertains, however, to diocesan councils in mission lands. Moreover, parish committees are instruments of the parish, and are therefore not lay apostolates.

4. Among the authors who question the system of standing committees, see William J. Bausch, *The Hands-On Parish* (Mystic, CT: Twenty-Third Publications, 1989), 89; Loughlan Sofield and Brenda Hermann, *Developing the Parish as a Community of Service* (New York: Le Jacq Publishing, 1984), 13; Robert R. Newsome, *The Ministering Parish: Methods and Procedures for Pastoral Organization* (New York and Ramsey, NJ: Paulist Press, 1982); and Robert G. Howes, *Creating an Effective Parish Pastoral Council* (Collegeville, MN: Liturgical Press, 1991). Rather than asking the pastoral council to coordinate a system of committees, Bausch (89) recommends meetings every two months of the "parish assembly," composed of the heads of ministries and organizations, to share information and to lobby with the pastor for particular projects.

5. See chap. 8 below, "How 'Pastoral' Are Councils?"

6. Previous parish pastoral council guidelines of Baltimore (21), Green Bay ("Norms," 6), and Seattle (33) have stated that the committees are "accountable" to the council. For Baltimore, see *Building One Body in*

Christ: The Ministry of the Parish Pastoral Council, with a letter from William Cardinal Keeler, Archbishop of Baltimore, first published, 1995; second printing (Baltimore: Archdiocese of Baltimore, 1997: 31 pages, plus 14 pages of appendices). For Green Bay, see *That All May Be One: Norms for Parish Pastoral Councils*, with a letter from Bishop Adam J. Maida, prepared by Rev. Larry Canavera and Sr. Luanne Smits, SSND (Diocese of Green Bay: Published by the Office of Parish Services, 1986; 10 pages of "Norms," together with a 33-page "Commentary and Resources" by Rev. Larry Canavera and Sr. Luanne Smits, SSND; and 51 pages of "Appendixes"). For Seattle, see *Policy and Guidelines for Parish Consultative Structures* (Archdiocese of Seattle: produced and published by the Planning and Research Department, 1990; reprinted, December, 1993).

     7. The pastoral council guidelines published by the dioceses of Charlotte (2008), Nashville (2004), Youngstown (2000), and Gaylord (2005), for example, envision a parish committee or commission structure coordinated by the pastoral council. See chap. 8 below, "How 'Pastoral' Are Councils?"

     8. For a good introduction to parish committee work, see Thomas Baker and Frank Ferrone, *Liturgy Committee Basics: A No-Nonsense Guide* (Washington, DC: Pastoral Press, 1985). The recruitment of volunteers, including committee members, to accomplish the parish mission is treated at length by William J. Bannon and Suzanne Donovan, *Volunteers and Ministry: A Manual for Developing Parish Volunteers* (New York and Ramsey, NJ: Paulist Press, 1983). The interplay of chairperson, facilitator, and recorder (in a non-Church milieu) is the topic of Michael Doyle and David Straus, *How to Make Meetings Work: The New Interactive Method*, second printing of the 1976 edition (New York: Jove Books, 1983). The human dynamics of a group and its leader are treated by Barbara J. Fleischer, *Facilitating for Growth: A Guide for Scripture Groups and Small Christian Communities* (Collegeville, MN: Liturgical Press, 1993). The *process* of committee work, especially the discernment of potential committee members and a non-adversarial way of promoting consensus, is outlined by Mary Benet McKinney, *Sharing Wisdom: A Process for Group Decision Making* (Allen, TX: Tabor Publishing, 1987). A spiritual approach to meetings which includes storytelling, theological reflection, discernment, and envisioning of the future is the focus of Charles M. Olsen, *Transforming Church Boards into Communities of Spiritual Leaders* (New York: Alban Institute, 1995). A very basic book about the importance of a clear goal and a well-planned agenda is Medard Laz, *Making Parish Meetings Work* (Notre Dame, IN: Ave Maria Press, 1997).

CHAPTER 4

Pastoral Council and Parish Staff

If a pastor has a good parish staff, why would he want a pastoral council? More and more Catholic parishes are very large and include a sizeable staff of expert laypeople.[1] The pastor of such a large parish can easily ask the staff members to investigate, reflect, and recommend to him their conclusions. Why should he even bother to consult a group of non-experts?

The simple answer is that wise pastors often consult about matters that do not require expert opinion. When a pastor seeks prudent advice about how to act on behalf of his parish in a changing situation, no expert has all the answers. The distinction between prudence and expertise goes back to Aristotle.[2] Wise pastors understand that some parish decisions require widespread support, and experts may not know the parish well enough to gauge that support. When a pastor's decision will affect the entire parish, he needs to know how it will do so, and tailor the decision to fit the community. In such a situation, experts may know their field of expertise better than they know parishioners. Their expertise may even prevent them from seeing the people's needs, and may skew their advice to the pastor.

To be sure, a good pastor recruits an expert staff for its special knowledge. He expects the parochial school principal to have studied educational administration. He wants a liturgy director with knowledge of music and sacramental theology. He would only hire a parish business manager familiar with accounting, budgets, and payroll. Often the pastor has to recruit widely, even from beyond the parish boundaries, to attract people with these special competencies. And when he has a technical question in these areas, he would be unwise to consult non-experts.

But when a pastor needs wise advice about a problem for which there is no one technical solution, the pastoral council can be an immense help. In order to appreciate the difference between the technical knowledge of the expert and the practical wisdom of the pastoral council, consider the following story about a pastor who relied on both.[3]

THE MULTIPURPOSE BUILDING

Not far from the birthplace of Richard Nixon lies the palm-studded parish of St. Paul of the Cross in La Mirada, California. St. Paul's had been planning to build a multipurpose hall for more than five years when Cardinal Roger Mahony, the Archbishop of Los Angeles, visited the parish in the spring of 1998. The cardinal had come to confirm the parish's young people. He listened with interest to plans for the new parish hall, and then raised a challenging question. Should not St. Paul's rebuild the parish's fifty-year-old church, the cardinal asked, before it constructed a multipurpose hall?

Cardinal Mahony's query raised a big question in the mind of Father Patrick Gannon. The pastor was in the final stages of architectural design for the multipurpose hall. Parishioners at St. Paul's had already contributed more than $200,000 to the project. Now Father Gannon had to rethink his plans. The parish wanted a hall, but also wanted to renovate the church.

Father Gannon turned to his key advisors, including the parish deacon and Tom Connolly, who was the chairman of the pastoral council. Connolly, an aerospace engineer, had been involved in planning for the new parish hall from the start. After meeting with these two advisers, Father Gannon decided to consult a larger and more representative group of parishioners. He invited the pastoral council and members of important parish committees (such as the building committee and finance council) to a two-hour meeting in the summer of 1998. He asked them to study the alternative proposed by Cardinal Mahony and consider whether the parish should continue its plan to construct a multipurpose building.

Father Gannon's decision to consult was significant. St. Paul's parishioners, he reasoned, would ultimately foot the bill for the project, whether it was a church renovation or a parish hall. Parishioners

should have a say about where their money goes. Meeting participants agreed that, since the parish had been fundraising more than
five years for a multipurpose hall, reassigning the funds to the construction of a new church building would put the good faith of
parishioners at risk.

Everyone, however, took seriously Cardinal Mahony's suggestion that St. Paul's rebuild its church. Indeed, parishioners had orig-
inally intended to do exactly that, but only after the construction of
the hall and not before. In light of the cardinal's suggestion, they
wondered whether they could do both projects simultaneously. So
the pastor, council chairman, and other key leaders consulted with
the architect, Victor Newlove, about the cost of building the hall
and renovating the church at the same time. The costs, however,
were prohibitive. St. Paul's could not afford to do what the cardinal
wanted and also build the parish hall.

The pastoral council and key leaders reviewed with Father
Gannon the results of their investigation. They affirmed that the
funds collected for the hall should not be reassigned to the construction of a new church. They advised Father Gannon that the parish
should hold fast to its original intention. Taking the council's advice,
he returned to archdiocesan officials and sought their permission.
After meeting with the archdiocesan building committee and financial officials, Father Gannon got a green light to build a hall. Regional
Bishop Joseph M. Sartoris, who had supported the construction of the
hall and actually made a contribution to the building fund, was present for its opening in April 2000. Parishioners affirmed the bishop's
suggestion to name it Gannon Hall, after their pastor.

THE ROLE OF THE COUNCIL

Pastoral council chairman Tom Connolly felt that the Gannon
Hall project had been a success, and attributed much of it to the trust
that existed between Father Gannon, the council, and other key
leaders. Father Gannon, Connolly said, had found himself in an awkward position. He had embarked on one plan, the plan to construct
a hall, and felt confident about it until Cardinal Mahony had suggested another possibility. The cardinal was not only the Archbishop
of Los Angeles, but also had the final say about archdiocesan con-

struction loans. Tom Connolly emphasized that everyone wanted to take the cardinal's suggestion about rebuilding the church seriously.

Father Gannon had to be both a good steward of his archdiocesan office and a good pastor. He needed to weigh his options and make a wise choice. The pastoral council helped him do so. Its members represented the common sense of parishioners. They did not want to be told that money saved for the parish hall would be spent on a different project. Moreover, the councillors realized that bringing the hall to a successful conclusion would enhance the good will of parishioners. Indeed, an attractive hall that could be rented out for wedding receptions and other events would be a source of parish income. Parishioner good will and additional income would be necessary for the next step, the renovation of the parish church itself.

But the council did not simply rely on its intuitions about parishioner sentiment. It also undertook a thorough investigation of the cardinal's suggestion. With the pastor, councillors met the archdiocesan building committee. They also met with Newlove, the architect, and estimated the cost of an expanded project encompassing both hall and church. They discussed the matter with archdiocesan financial officials. And they sounded out parish committees, such as the building committee and finance council. Their cooperation, support, and leadership, Tom Connolly said, were essential. Then and only then did the pastoral council make its recommendations to Father Gannon.

Father Gannon also felt that the construction of the parish hall had been a successful venture, and he attributed much of the success to the pastoral council. The members had helped him in a very delicate situation. He had the difficult task of integrating the wishes of his archbishop and his parishioners. The fact that he ultimately won approval for the project and completed it testifies to the soundness of his council's advice. Top archdiocesan officials appreciated the way the pastoral council had studied the feasibility of the project. And Cardinal Mahony, by extending to St. Paul's a $700,000 construction loan, himself acknowledged the council's wisdom.

PLANNING BY EXPERTS

The Gannon Hall project succeeded because it was based on reliable knowledge and good advice. The search for such knowledge and advice is precisely the role of every pastoral council. Such councils are to investigate pastoral matters, reflect on them, and reach conclusions which are then recommended to pastors. St. Paul's parish pastoral council was doing precisely what councils everywhere are supposed to do.

Someone may well ask, however, whether the pastoral council at St. Paul's ought to have played such a decisive role. After all, it might be said, the council members were not experts in finance, architecture, or archdiocesan policy. Should Father Gannon not have deferred rather to the opinions of the experts?

In order to answer this question about pastoral decision-making, we have to distinguish between the importance of expert opinion and practical wisdom. Experts can tell the decision-making pastor what is best as a general rule and in most cases. Practical wisdom seeks, from among the many things an expert might recommend, what is prudent in an actual parish situation. Both kinds of knowledge—the expert and the practically wise—are important.[4]

Archdiocesan finance officials could tell Father Gannon how to budget for construction and schedule the repayment of a loan. The architect, Victor Newlove, could advise him about the building of church halls and how to get the most for his construction dollar. But these experts did not know the parish as well as the parishioners themselves. They could not anticipate the will of the parish community, predict all of its construction needs, or gauge what is appropriate in the parish's own situation. Father Gannon needed this practical wisdom as well as expert opinion. For that reason he consulted his pastoral council. Councillors consulted the experts, yes, but they had something that the experts could not provide. They had knowledge of the parish itself.

PLANNING BY COUNCILS

Many are tempted to think that pastoral planning is something of an abstract exercise. They see it as merely the formal application to a concrete parish situation of theoretical principles. This application, they believe, should be performed by experts—architectural, financial, liturgical, what have you—on behalf of the parish community. Key decisions are to be made only by those with specific training in technical professions. Ordinary parishioners, according to this view, should have no authoritative role.

The construction of Gannon Hall at St. Paul of the Cross, however, suggests that this view of pastoral planning is shortsighted. Were pastoral planning only the abstract application of general principles, there would be no need for discussion. But in fact the cardinal's suggestion spurred the council on to plan in earnest. Had Cardinal Mahony not spoken, the parish would have proceeded without testing its assumptions as thoroughly as it did. It had assumed that it could not afford to simultaneously build the hall and renovate the church. At Cardinal Mahony's prompting, the council tested that assumption by consulting the architect and financial officials. The cardinal's suggestion motivated a more profound study, deeper reflection, and more effective planning.

Some leaders fear popular participation in decision making. They surround themselves with experts and distrust the voices of ordinary people. But that was not Father Gannon's way in the construction of his parish hall. To be sure, he relied upon the expert advice of the architect. And he frequently consulted with the parish business manager and the parochial school principal. But he also appreciated the importance of the pastoral council. By consulting it, he not only invited its reflection on the opinion of experts, but gained prudent insights from the common sense of his own congregation.

The pastoral council can investigate a situation, not from the viewpoint of an expert, but from the viewpoint of the parish community. To be sure, good councillors do consult experts. The council at St. Paul's consulted the archdiocesan finance council as well as other experts, architect Newlove, and the parish's own building committee and finance council. This is part of the councillors' duty to investigate thoroughly.

But the council's main contribution is not expertise or scientific knowledge. The members acknowledge that there will be a variety of opinions within the parish, and they try to gather them impartially. After they have studied the situation, they can reflect on their findings. They can analyze them, discern what they mean, and weigh the consequences. This is the work of practical wisdom. And when a pastor has participated in the council's deliberations, raising his own questions and listening to the various answers, he knows that the members have taken his own doubts into consideration.

SEVEN RULES FOR PASTORAL PLANNING BY COUNCILS

Let us conclude this chapter by proposing seven rules for pastoral planning by councils. These rules integrate a number of the insights we have gained so far about the distinctly "pastoral" nature of the pastoral council.

1. Plan with the pastor. If he does not believe in the plan, he will not accept it or implement it wholeheartedly.

2. Plan with parishioners. If the council does not give parishioners regular opportunities to give advice, they will not support the plan.

3. Expect course corrections. Responsible opposition to a plan provides valuable knowledge of which the council must take account.

4. Report regularly. Inform parishioners of the status of the plan, especially of changes made in response to parishioner advice.

5. Cast a wide net. When you think you have studied a matter thoroughly, publish the results. You will inevitably discover new viewpoints that need to be considered.

6. Talk to experts but reserve judgment. Experts can tell you what is generally true, but not always what will apply in your situation.

7. Do not hurry the process. The council that plans thoroughly will reach sound recommendations that pastors are likely to accept.

Good pastoral councillors are not chosen because of their technical expertise in theology, counseling, or management. No, they are chosen for their practical wisdom. That is the ability to understand a situation and choose a course of action that is prudent, i.e., appropriate for a community and its leaders. Father Gannon found that ability in his council. His consultation with them was successful because it followed the seven rules above.

NOTES

1. Regarding the size of parish staffs, David DeLambo says that there are "30,632 lay parish ministers working at least 20 hours per week" and that

they can be found in 68 percent of U.S. parishes. See DeLambo, *Lay Parish Ministers: A Study of Emerging Leadership*, a study conducted for the Committee on the Laity of the United States Conference of Catholic Bishops with major support of the Lilly Endowment, Inc., and additional funding from the Emerging Models of Pastoral Excellence Project (New York: National Pastoral Life Center, 2005), 44.

Francis Kelly Scheets estimates that "corporate" parishes (those which number more than 3000 Catholics in more than 1200 households) make up 32 percent of all U.S. Catholic parishes but register over 71 percent of U.S. Catholics. See Scheets, "Parish Information Systems—Resources for Ministry," chap. 9 of *The Parish Management Handbook: A Practical Guide for Pastors, Administrators, and Other Parish Leaders*, ed. Charles E. Zech (Mystic, CT: Twenty-Third Publications, 2003), 196–217; 200 quoted here.

2. Aristotle described *prudence* as *phronesis* or "practical wisdom," and his word for *expert opinion* was *episteme* or "scientific knowledge." In Book Six of his *Nicomachean Ethics*, Aristotle referred to *phronesis* as the ability to act rationally, and he defined it as "a truthful rational characteristic of acting in matters involving what is good" for human beings (Aristotle, *Nicomachean Ethics*, translated with an introduction and notes by Martin Ostwald [Indianapolis, IN: Bobbs-Merrill, 1962], VI.5, 154). One cannot prove by empirical means how best to act, so instead of seeking a demonstration, those with practical wisdom deliberate among different courses of action.

Distinct from practical wisdom is scientific knowledge or *episteme*. The objects of such knowledge cannot be other than what they are, and the scientific expert seeks them for their own sake by a process of demonstration. Indeed, Aristotle defined *scientific knowledge* as "a capacity for demonstration" (ibid., VI.3, 151). Scientific knowledge is the province of experts such as the pastor's staff. A purely scientific approach is preferable when one seeks permanent truths that add to an expert's body of knowledge. In the pastoral council the pastor seeks practical wisdom. Councillors gain it by deliberating about how to act in a changing situation.

3. The story is based on Mark F. Fischer, "The Pastor, the Experts, and the Pastoral Council," *Today's Parish* 34:3 (March 2002): 12–15.

4. As Aristotle noted, scientific knowledge stems from correct reasoning and is morally neutral. Practical wisdom aims at choosing the good and has a moral dimension. "If the choice is to be good, the reasoning must be true and the desire correct." Aristotle, *Nicomachean Ethics*, VI.2, 148. For a discussion of Aristotle and the pastoral council, see Mark F. Fischer, *Pastoral Councils in Today's Catholic Parish* (Mystic, CT: Twenty-Third Publications, 2001), 144–145.

CHAPTER 5

Pastoral and Finance Council

No Vatican document describes the relation between the parish pastoral and parish finance council. But if we understand the pastoral council as the one that aids the apostolate of the pastor, we can discover general principles that ought to govern its relation to the finance council, as the following story suggests.

In 2005 the *Vista Clara Union* announced the opening of a new subdivision within the city limits. "Village on the Green," the paper said, would eventually include more than one thousand attached and detached residences, all designed by a well-known developer based in Dallas. The developer called them "luxury home sites" and the newspaper reprinted architectural drawings showing the homes as they would look when the landscaping had matured and the trees had grown. As more and more homes were sold at the Village, St. Philip's Catholic Church in Vista Clara began to enjoy a slow but steady increase in Mass attendance. Father Leo Vicente, the pastor, was happy to see the increase. For several years he had felt that St. Philip's was outgrowing the parish church, which had opened in 1967, and the church hall, constructed at the same time. With an increase in parishioners from the Village, he felt, the parish's income would grow, and he could begin a building campaign for a new church and hall at St. Philip's (the names in this chapter have been changed).

In order to lay the groundwork for an eventual campaign, Father Vicente invited the parish pastoral council to begin assessing the parish's overall needs. At a meeting on March 15, 2005, he sketched the kind of planning that he hoped the council would do. He asked the members to help him produce a newsletter for distribution to parishioners. The newsletter would describe, first of all, the current situation of the parish—finances, facilities, and demographics. It would show that the number of parishioners is growing and that (throughout the diocese) the number of priests able to serve them is shrinking. In addition, the newsletter would propose how an expansion of the church and other facilities would benefit the parish. By the end of the meeting, the councillors had made a preliminary plan for the newsletter and each member had volunteered to draft a different section.

THE PRELIMINARY REPORTS

By the June 28 meeting, the members had completed their preliminary reports and assembled an incomplete draft of the parish renovation newsletter entitled "The Future of St. Philip's Church." The report had five sections:

1. Population Growth

This first section of the newsletter, written by a parishioner and city planner named Fides Medina, estimated a 15 percent annual growth of the parish population. The members complimented her work but some wished that Fides would have distinguished between city growth in general and the growth of St. Philip's Church in particular. The city would grow, they said, but would the parish grow at the same rate?

2. Facilities Needs

Carlos Gomez, an enthusiastic businessman who served as chairman of the council, said that he had contacted the parish business manager. The business manager has a list of regular facility users—that, is, a list of those who regularly use the church hall and school auditorium—and will provide it to the council. Regular users might be willing to pay a fee, Gomez said, if they knew that the money would be dedicated to a renovation of church facilities.

3. Personnel Needs

This part was written by Fred Billings, a permanent deacon and retired man who also serves on the parish finance council. Billings was cautious about publishing information about the parish. His draft report did not include specific figures about the size of the parish staff. The other councillors asked him about this. Billings replied that parishioners did not need specific numbers to know that the lay staff would grow and the parish would have a single priest.

4. Renovation of the Church

Cecilia Serrano drafted this section of the future newsletter. She listed a number of potential improvements, above all an expansion of the church's seating area. With fewer priests, she said, there might be fewer Masses, but these Masses would be heavily attended.

5. School Renovation

José Lopez reported that he had telephoned Don Hulton, the principal of St. Philip's elementary school. Hulton replied with a question. He asked whether the council was trying to ascertain "future needs" or a "future wish list." The two men had made an appointment for a future conversation.

At the end of the five preliminary reports, Father Vicente felt that the council was right on track. The members were drafting a parish newsletter that, when published, would indicate the need for improving the parish's facilities. Father Vicente hoped that the newsletter would prompt people to begin thinking about the need for fundraising.

DIFFERENCES REGARDING THE TWO COUNCILS

Carlos Gomez, the chairman, was in high spirits. An optimist about the future who is always enthusiastic about plans for growth, Gomez quickly made three observations. First, he thanked Fides Medina for her population estimates. They are scientific projections, he said, and based on city statistics. He said that they will translate into a 15 percent growth in parish income per year. Gomez's second comment was that the parish's budget ought to reflect those estimates. The budget, he said, should assign the new income to the capital improvements fund. Finally, Gomez suggested that regular users of church facilities should pay a users' fee to help cover the renovation cost. People will be willing to do so, he repeated, if they knew that the additional income would support the cost of parish renovation.

While Gomez was speaking, Fred Billings, the permanent deacon, shifted uncomfortably in his seat. When Gomez was finished, Billings spoke up.

"We need to remember," Billings said to Carlos Gomez, "that this is a pastoral council, not a finance council."

"Do you mean it is less important than the finance council?" asked Gomez.

"No, but it's not the prerogative of the pastoral council to make judgments about future income and how the parish should account for it," said the deacon. "That belongs to the finance council."

"I wasn't making any judgments, Fred," Gomez replied. "I was simply expressing an opinion. The city statistics suggest that the parish will grow. The increased income ought to go into the capital budget. The pastoral council needs to anticipate that."

"I disagree," said Billing. "The finance council has a specific formula for estimating parish income. It's based on a record of past income. These speculations about future growth, Carlos, simply aren't relevant."

"Not relevant?" asked Carlos. "Father Leo has asked us to assess parish needs and propose how to meet them," Gomez said. "That means how to pay for them."

"But you can't simply assume, on the basis of city projections, that parish income will grow by a certain percent," said Billings with exasperation. "Estimating parish income is an administrative question that belongs to the finance council."

"Since when is parish administration off-limits for the pastoral council?" Gomez countered. "Everybody knows that the city is growing, and it's perfectly safe to assume that the parish will grow too."

"Administration belongs to the finance council," Billings repeated.

"And policy is the province of the pastoral council," Gomez shot back. "We need a policy about asking users of parish facilities to pay a fee—or is that too much of an administrative question for you?"

Father Vicente intervened at that point. He had been happy to see the pastoral councillors take on the project of creating a parish newsletter about renovation. But he had not anticipated the tension between the pastoral and finance councils. He knew that he had to define more clearly what he was asking of each council. Carlos Gomez had common sense, but he was more enthusiastic than cautious, and he did not know the parish's process for budgeting. The process was complicated but reliable, and Deacon Fred Billings was an expert at it. Billings' assertion, however, that administration was the exclusive province of the finance council, seemed a little extreme. Father Vicente was glad to shift the topic of conversation to another matter.

OFFICIAL TEACHING

The story about the disagreement over the role of pastoral and finance councils at St. Philip's Church has been fictionalized, but it illustrates a real problem. What is the Church's teaching about pastoral and finance councils at the parish level? There is very little Vatican documentation about the two. The Code of Canon Law devotes a single canon to each. Regarding the purpose of pastoral councils, canon 536 simply states that they "assist in fostering pastoral activity."[1] In a later chapter we will examine this canon at length. For the moment, it is enough to note that that canon 536 does not even allude to the finance council.

We read about the finance council in the very next canon, canon 537. It too is very brief:

> In each parish there is to be a finance council which is governed, in addition to universal law, by norms issued by the diocesan bishop and in which the Christian faithful, selected according to these same norms, are to assist the pastor in the administration of the goods of the parish, without prejudice to the prescript of canon 532.[2]

The reference to universal law, and especially to canon 532, underscores the advisory nature of the finance council. It advises the pastor. He "represents the parish according to the norm of law."[3] The finance council's role is "to assist the pastor in the administration" of parish goods. Canon 537 does not explain how the council is to do this. It merely says that norms issued by the diocesan bishop govern the council's actions.[4] Canons 536 and 537 certainly do not spell out the relations between the two councils, except to say that one assists in fostering pastoral activity and the other assists in the administration of goods.[5] In short, canon law leaves relations between the two councils in obscurity.

Finance councils, we read, are governed by norms issued by the local bishop. One might assume that local bishops have clarified the relation between the finance and pastoral councils. But diocesan publications are not of one mind. Some have insisted upon the pre-eminence of the pastoral council. They state that it decides priorities for the parish. Financial accountability is one of the parish's missions, according to this view, and the pastoral council oversees it.[6] Other diocesan publications, however, regard the pastoral and finance councils on an even footing. Both serve the pastor, who consults them about different matters.[7] Pastoral councils deal with pastoral matters, from this perspective, and finance councils with financial.

The late Bishop John Keating of Arlington even went so far as to suggest that pastoral councils should have nothing to do with parish administration. He argued that, according to canon 537, the administration of parish goods belongs exclusively to the finance council. From this he drew the conclusion that temporal matters belong to the finance council, and pastoral matters belong to the pastoral council. No pastoral council, he maintained, should deal with parish administration.[8]

Bishop Keating's view proved unpersuasive, however, because it unduly restricted the scope of the pastoral council. That scope has been consistently described as "pastoral matters." Pastors will consult about practical matters that are important to them. To be sure, Vatican documents distinguish between the exercise of jurisdiction or governing power and the consultative role of the pastoral council. Councils, the documents say, do not govern. But that does not mean that questions of governance or administration are off-limits for the pastoral council. Indeed, the Congregation for the Clergy's 1973 "Circular Letter on 'Pastoral Councils' " made this explicit. It stated that pastoral councils may consider acts of governance that belong specifically to the pastor as the one who legally acts on behalf of the parish.[9] Few canonists would admit Bishop Keating's sharp distinction between pastoral matters and parish administration.[10] To say, as Bishop Keating did, that the administration of the parish does not fall within the scope of "pastoral matters," is to curtail the pastor's freedom to consult as he sees fit.

The Church's official teaching does not sufficiently explain the relation between pastoral and finance councils. Vatican documents, diocesan publications, and scholarly articles do not express a clear consensus.

THE CORRECT STARTING POINT

What then is the correct starting point in assessing the relationship between the pastoral and finance councils? The starting point is the pastor. He is the one who consults the two councils. They are not branches of government, like the Office of Strategic Planning and the Office of the Treasury, whose duties are regulated by law. No, the pastoral and finance councils are consultative bodies. They do not work independently of the pastor. They do not enact policy on their own. If we want to know how the two should relate to one another, we need to determine how the pastor consults them and why.

Earlier, we noted that pastoral and finance councils cannot be distinguished purely on the basis of their subject matter. To be sure, pastoral councils focus on "pastoral" matters. This refers, however, to matters that pertain to the pastor. Pastoral does not mean topics that are "spiritual" rather than "temporal." Rather, it has to do with the pastor's leadership of the parish. Finance councils, we said, assist the pastor in the administration of parish goods. Diocesan norms commonly state that they help the pastor estimate income and develop a budget. This has "pastoral" consequences because the pastor is the parish's legal representative. Administration is pastoral, and pastoral includes administration. The stewardship of the parish's resources, for example, straddles both fields.[11] Thus we cannot simply say that pastoral councils deal exclusively with pastoral issues, and that finance councils confine their efforts to the administrative (in contrast to the pastoral) field. Pastoral and administrative are not separate areas of inquiry. They overlap.

So how do we distinguish between the pastoral and the finance council? The key, I said, is that the pastor consults both of them. He consults two different councils because he seeks something different from each. The distinction does not stem from different subject matters, i.e., the pastoral and the administrative. No, the distinction arises because the pastor seeks different types of knowledge, uses different methods of inquiry, and invites the different gifts of his councillors.

AN ARISTOTELIAN SOLUTION

This effort to distinguish between the two councils is grounded on very old principles, the principles laid down by Aristotle. In book VI of the *Nicomachean Ethics*, Aristotle distinguished among the ways by which one pursues the truth. One way concerns what is always and everywhere true, and Aristotle called it *pure science* or *knowledge*.[12] It can be compiled in a book or guideline. It comprises general principles upon which experts agree. Aristotle's pure science or knowledge is applicable to parish finance councils. With their focus on the disciplines of finance and accounting, they offer the pastor a kind of scientific knowledge.

There is another way to the truth, however, that does not seek general principles. It seeks what is best in a concrete situation. Aristotle called it *practical wisdom*.[13] It is a particular kind of truth, the truth about contingent matters. It follows no general rule, for it is the truth about how one should act in a particular situation. The situation in which we find ourselves is always changing. There can be no one rule about how to act. People seek this practical wisdom by means of dialogue. Pastoral councils have an affinity with Aristotle's practical wisdom. They seek this prudent knowledge, because they deliberate about the practical activity of parishes.

Aristotle's distinction between practical wisdom and science, in short, helps us to distinguish between finance and pastoral councils. By linking finance councils to the science of accounting, and by linking pastoral council to practical wisdom, we have a way of understanding the distinctive gift of each. We can distinguish between the type of knowledge that each council seeks, between their methods, and between the gifts of councillors. Let me say a word about each.

Types of Knowledge

Science, for Aristotle, does not refer to the "scientific method" as we know it today. It is not merely the work of formulating hypotheses and testing them in a laboratory. To science (in the Aristotelian sense) belongs every kind of knowledge that is always and everywhere true. It is the knowledge of the expert. Science is the knowledge of those things that cannot be other than what they are. In the finance council, we speak of the science of accounting.

Practical wisdom, on the other hand, has to do with action. Practical wisdom concerns deeds that we may or may not want to do. People with practical wisdom, says Aristotle, have a capacity for seeing what is good. The good that they see is not an abstraction, but rather the best choice of action in a given situation. For pastoral councillors, it is contingent on the pastor and the parish. Those with practical wisdom are able to rightly judge how matters stand with a particular community. A parish can make many different choices about religious education, liturgy, social justice, parish renovation, and care for the elderly. Yet it is obvious that no parish can do everything. That is where practical wisdom comes in. The council with practical wisdom helps a pastor decide what the parish ought to do with limited resources.

So finance councils are scientific, in Aristotle's sense of the word, and pastoral councils are practically wise. The Aristotelian distinction enables us to distinguish between them. But what are the consequences for the way the two councils run?

The Method of the Two Councils

Aristotle stated that scientific knowledge can be demonstrated and taught. If we apply his insight to the finance council, we see the council's fundamentally scientific nature. Finance councils help a pastor prepare the parish budget. The councillors project next year's income from a history of the last years' income. This is the basis for the following year's payroll, operating expenses, and capital improvements. The goal of the finance council is straightforward. It is to demonstrate the parish's finances and to predict what will happen if income and expenses are as projected. The basic principles of accounting are fixed, unchangeable, and (as Aristotle would say) scientific.

In the pastoral council, however, there is no "scientific" way to proceed. Without a doubt, pastoral councils amass facts, study issues, and calculate with regard to worthwhile ends. They proceed scientifically in the sense that their goal is knowledge. But the knowledge that pastoral councils seek is not the demonstrably scientific knowledge of finance councils. It is rather a kind of wisdom: the knowledge of what is good for a community and the ability to reason about what the community desires. "Reasoning must affirm what desire pursues," wrote Aristotle.[14] The pastoral council must hold up to the light of reason the desires of the parish community, affirming what is practically wise and recommending it to the pastor.

Aristotle's distinction between science and practical wisdom helps us to distinguish between the methods of the two councils. Finance councils proceed by demonstration, that is, by showing and making clear.[15] They manifest the financial reality of the parish, projecting it into the future. They demonstrate this financial reality on the basis of scientific principles of accounting.

Pastoral councils, by contrast, proceed by deliberation.[16] They have no fixed-and-firm scientific method. Why? Because what they deliberate about—the shifting needs of the parish—follows no unchangeable rules. Pastoral councils apply a capacity for seeing the community's good. This capacity, practical wisdom, enables them to consider a number of actions, all of which are good in themselves. Their wisdom is "practical" because it aims at choice and action. Pastoral councillors choose, from among all the good things the parish could possibly do, what it should actually do.

The Gifts of Councillors

Pastoral and finance councils differ in their tasks. Moreover, the different councillors themselves ought to have different gifts. Aristotle sketches the differing gifts of those who pursue science and practical wisdom. His sketch has consequences for the selection of council members. Finance council members should have expert knowledge. They should be familiar with the science of accounting, should be able to rigorously demonstrate the parish's finances, and should be able to express their conclusions to the pastor. Financial knowledge is the primary criterion for selecting finance councillors.

Pastoral council members, however, need not be scientific experts. Their gift is deliberation. They should know the parish. They should be able to judge how it will respond to new initiatives. They should be able to express their opinions well, and to listen attentively to the opinions of others in a dispassionate way. By controlling their passions, as Aristotle said, the wise preserve the ability to judge correctly.[17] Above all, they should be able to synthesize the various opinions, clarifying them and making sound recommendations. Their goal is not to gain an advantage for one group at the expense of another, but to seek the common good.

Ordinary parishioners can discern who among their peers has the gift of deliberation. It is wise, as we shall see in the next chapter, to involve parishioners in the choice of pastoral councillors. But no guideline suggests a popular election of finance councillors. They are experts, and should be chosen for their expert ability. Not everyone can serve as pastoral and finance councillors. People without scientific knowledge of accounting should decline the invitation to be finance council members. Those who are impatient with discussion, who lack the ability to consider all sides of a question, and who want to impulsively get on with the work of the parish, need not apply for the pastoral council.

RESOLVING THE PROBLEM AT ST. PHILIP'S CHURCH

Earlier we had dramatized the conflict between Carlos Gomez, the chairperson of the pastoral council at St. Philip's Church, and Fred Billings, the deacon who sat on both the pastoral and the finance councils. Carlos, working with research done by the City of Clara Vista, had speculated that the parish population and income would rise by 15 percent. He argued that the parish income projections should reflect that figure. Finally, he recommended that the parish charge a fee for the use of its facilities, with the proceeds going to a renovation fund. These recommendations, he believed, are the proper work of the pastoral council.

Deacon Fred Billings disagreed. He claimed that the pastoral council was usurping the rights of the finance council. To the finance council, he told Carlos Gomez, belongs the responsibility for estimating parish income. That is a technical job for accountants and people with financial expertise, he said, not for laypersons. In his mind, parish administration in general belongs to the finance council, not the pastoral council.

How can we adjudicate between Carlos Gomez and Fred Billings? We saw in this chapter that an analysis of canon law will not suffice. Instead, we began with the fundamental principle that the pastor consults both the finance and pastoral councils. Pastors must decide what they are to consult about. The tension between the two councils cannot be resolved by assigning one subject matter, the "pastoral," and another subject matter, the "administrative," to each council. No—pastoral and administrative overlap. So the pastor has to make choices about what he will consult about.

To help the pastor make sound choices, the general principles laid down by Aristotle prove useful. He distinguished between the types of knowledge, method, and personal gifts needed for the pursuit of scientific knowledge and practical wisdom. This distinction clarifies the tensions between the pastoral and finance councils of St. Philip's Church. Carlos Gomez, the pastoral council chairman was not prudent in his assessment of the statistics about population growth in Vista Clara. He assumed that, because the city expected a 15 percent rise in population, St. Philip's could assume the same population growth. Moreover, Carlos argued that the parish should plan for a 15 percent expansion of income. This was wishful thinking. Father Vicente should have said, "I rely upon the finance council alone to help me estimate parish income."

Deacon Fred Billings was right to say that pastoral councils should not estimate income. That is a science (in the Aristotelian sense), a science based on a careful analysis of the parish's income history. It should be left to financial experts. But Billings overreacted to Carlos Gomez when he said that "Administration belongs to the finance council." That comment echoed the discredited interpretation of Bishop Keating, namely, that pastoral councils should not consider administrative questions. Father Vicente should have intervened. He should have said, "I rely upon the pastoral council to weigh the consequences of new policies, and I would like it to study the possibility of charging a fee for the use of parish facilities."

In conclusion, the consultative pastor who relies on his two councils ought to navigate with both of them. They are not two agencies of government, but two sources of knowledge. He navigates best, I believe, when he distinguishes between the type of knowledge that each council offers, between their methods, and between the gifts of councillors. The pastoral council aims at practical wisdom through deliberation. The finance council pursues a scientific approach to budgeting and accounting. The wise pastor recognizes the excellence of each council, and asks what each is suited to give. The value of the two councils depends on the excellence of the councillors. The next chapter will show how to attract and recruit good pastoral council members.

NOTES

1. *Code of Canon Law*, c. 536. Cited according to John P. Beal, James A. Coriden, and Thomas J. Green, Editors, *New Commentary on the Code of Canon Law* (New York and Mahwah, NJ: Paulist Press, 2000), 708.

2. Ibid., c. 537, p. 710.

3. Ibid., c. 532, p. 703. C. 532 states, "In all juridic affairs the pastor represents the parish according to the norm of law. He is to take care that the goods of the parish are administered according to the norm of canons 1281–1288." These canons limit the scope of official parish administrators (c. 1281), state that such administrators are bound by the Church's law (c. 1282), require that they be good stewards (c. 1283), list the duties of the good steward (c. 1284), allow administrators to make charitable donations in the Church's name (c. 1285), require them to act with due regard for social justice (c. 1286), bind them to render a faithful account of their ministry (c. 1286), and forbid them from litigating without the bishop's permission (c. 1288).

4. Every bishop may publish finance council norms for his diocese. In 1995, the U.S. Bishops provided a framework for diocesan financial accounting. See the Committee on Budget and Finance, National Conference of Catholic Bishops, U.S. Catholic Conference, "Diocesan Internal Controls: A Framework" (available online at http://www.usccb.org/finance/internal.shtml). The diocesan framework is applicable to parish accounting, and its comments on the diocesan finance council are relevant to the parish finance council.

5. John A. Renken, in his commentary on c. 537, states that the roles of the pastoral and finance councils are "distinct," the one dedicated to "planning" and the other to "the administration of parochial goods." He adds that "Their roles are distinct, and each must be careful to retain its proper focus should they collaborate with one another." Renken, "Parishes and Pastors [cc. 515–544]," in the *New Commentary on the Code of Canon Law*, 711.

6. In Milwaukee, Harrisburg, and St. Louis, pastoral councils have taken precedence over finance councils. The Archdiocese of Milwaukee's *Parish Committee Ministry* (1991) stated that the finance committee "does not decide priorities for the parish—that is the responsibility of the parish council" (46). It made the finance council a standing committee of the pastoral council. The Diocese of Harrisburg's *Parish Council Policy and Guidelines* (1985) stated that financial administration is one of the "missions" of the parish, and that the parish council "supersedes every other parish organization, board, and committee" (8), including the finance council. The Harrisburg document and the Archdiocese of St. Louis' *Guidelines*

for the Ministry of Parish Councils (1985) insisted that finance council members be appointed after consultation with the parish council, thereby ensuring the pastoral council's primacy. In these dioceses, the pastoral council has primacy. For a further discussion, see Mark F. Fischer, "Should Finance Councils Answer to Parish Councils?" *Today's Parish* 26:3 (March 1994): 21–23, 32.

7. Documents from Los Angeles, Richmond, and Cleveland put the pastoral and finance councils on an even footing. The 1991 *Parish Pastoral Council Guidelines* for the Archdiocese of Los Angeles described the responsibility of the finance council as "fiscal stewardship" and made it somewhat independent of the pastoral council. "While the Finance Council has responsibility for the stewardship of parish financial resources," we read, "it is not the role of the Finance Council to recommend directions, priorities, or programs other than those related to its delegation namely, fiscal stewardship" (18). Richmond's 1991 *Norms for Parish Finance Councils* and Cleveland's 1991 *Parish Finance Council Policy* also agree that finance and pastoral councils should cooperate, because finance councils are not standing committees of the parish council.

8. Keating, "Consultation in the Parish," *Origins* 14:17 (October 11, 1984): 257, 259–266. Keating's viewpoint was seconded by Peter Kim and Orville Griese. See Peter Kim Se-Mang, *Parish Councils on Mission: Co-Responsibility and Authority among Pastoral and Parishioners* (Kuala Lumpur: Benih Publisher, 1991), 48; and Orville Griese, "The New Code of Canon Law and Parish Councils," *Homiletic and Pastoral Review* 85:4 (January 1985), 47–53, 53 cited here.

9. Vatican Council II's *Decree on Bishops* (*Christus Dominus*), no. 27, said that diocesan pastoral councils are "cooperators of the bishop in the governing of the diocese." It recommended cooperation between pastoral councils and senates of priests. The Council's *Decree on the Ministry and Life of Priests* (*Presbyterorum ordinis*) suggested that the assignment of "management" to the Senate of Priests does not remove the topic of "administration" from the DPC agenda. See Vatican Council II, *Presbyterorum Ordinis* (Decree on the Ministry and Life of Priests, December 7, 1965), no. 7, translated by Archbishop Joseph Cunnane, of Tuam, and revised by Michael Mooney and Enda Lyons of St. Jarlath's College, Tuam, County Galway, in in *Vatican Council II*, ed. Austin Flannery, vol. 1: *The Conciliar and Post-Conciliar Documents*, 877.

The Vatican II teaching about cooperation between pastoral councils and senates of priests was amplified in Pope Paul VI's apostolic letter of 1966, *Ecclesiae Sanctae I*. It stated (at no. 15) that the priests' senate advises the bishop in matters that pertain to the exercise of jurisdiction or governing power. Bishops may consult their pastoral councils, however, about such jurisdictional matters. Emphasizing this point, the Congregation for the Clergy's 1973 "Circular Letter on Pastoral 'Councils' " (*Omnes Christifideles*) stated: "Nothing prevents the pastoral council, however, from considering questions requiring mandates of a jurisdictional act for execution and proposing suggestions regarding them to the bishop, for in such a case the bishop will consider the matter and make his decision after hearing the priests' senate, if the case requires" (no. 9). By extension, nothing prevents the parish pastoral council from considering questions related to parish administration.

10. About the breadth of the category of "pastoral," the late James H. Provost wrote: "Nothing, therefore, escapes the category of *pastoral* if it truly pertains to the Church." See Provost, "Canon Law and the Role of Consultation," *Origins* 18:47 (May 4, 1989): 793, 795–799, at 798. John Renken has opposed the preoccupation of parish pastoral councils with administration, but conceded that "we can imagine some single issue may involve both [finance and pastoral] councils." See Renken, "Pastoral Councils: Pastoral Planning and Dialogue among the People of God," *The Jurist* 53 (1993): 132–154, 150 cited here. William Dalton has called for parish pastoral councils to be more pastoral, but he gave them the administrative task of coordinating parish activities. See Dalton, "Parish Councils or Parish Pastoral Councils?" *Studia Canonica* 22 (1988): 169–185, 174 cited here. Sidney J. Marceaux has argued that efforts to restrict the scope of the parish pastoral council in light of the 1983 Code are superseded by the broad scope granted to pastoral councils by Vatican II's *Decree on Bishops*, which "carries a greater force of law" than the Code. See Marceaux, "The Pastoral Council," (JCD diss., Pontifical University of Studies at St. Thomas Aquinas in the City, 1980), 143. These authors were discussed in Fischer, "What Was Vatican II's Intent?"

11. Charles E. Zech, "Developing Stewards in a Parish Setting," chap. 7 of *The Parish Management Handbook*, ed. Charles E. Zech (Mystic, CT: Twenty-Third Publications, 2003), 154–172.

12. Aristotle described "pure science" or "knowledge" (*episteme*) in *Nicomachean Ethics*, Book VI.3.

13. Aristotle described "practical wisdom" (*phronesis*) in *Nicomachean Ethics*, Book VI.5 and VI.8–13.

14. Ibid., VI.2.

15. Ibid., VI.3.

16. Ibid., VI.9.

17. Ibid., VI.5.

CHAPTER 6

Selecting Pastoral Council Members

In chapter 2, we met Father Jim Stehly, the pastor of St. Mary Magdalen Church. Father Stehly had invited his council to study the parish's efforts on behalf of social justice. He was contemplating the establishment of a new social justice committee at St. Mary Magdalen in response to a recommendation from the archdiocesan synod. It said that every parish should have an outreach ministry for the needy. But when the pastoral council looked into the matter, it found that St. Mary Magdalen already had twenty-one groups whose parish work included social justice activities. The council did not recommend the establishment of a new committee, but urged Father Stehly to support existing efforts and publicize them better. The pastor was grateful. Had he started a new social justice committee, he might have seemed unappreciative and even disrespectful toward the parish's existing social justice efforts.

The council that assisted Father Stehly in the years 2004–2005 was composed of eight members. Four of the existing eight had already served longer than their three-year term. Those members were the remnant of the council that the pastor had established in 2002. The members of the original council were chosen by Father Stehly to represent the parish's different ethnic groups and organizations. They believed that they represented those groups and organizations, but they understood representation in various ways. Some felt that they were to be advocates for the particular ministry from which they were drawn. Others thought that they were to draw the pastor's attention to a particular culture or linguistic group. But as the months passed, and more and more time at meetings was devoted to reports from this group or that, many members became discouraged. Attendance dropped. Father Stehly knew that he had to replenish the council membership, but he was not sure how to do so.

The pastor faced three questions. First and foremost was the criterion for councillor selection. With three years of pastoral council experience, Father Stehly knew better what he sought in a good councillor than when he began. Another question was about the size of the council and the representative nature of the members. His approach in 2002, which was to select people himself on the basis of their culture and their membership in organizations, had not proven successful. His third question was about the method of selection. He wanted a method that would attract a large number of people and involve the parish. Let us see how Father Stehly answered his questions about the criterion, representative nature, and selection of councillors.

THE CRITERION FOR SELECTION

The falling-off in attendance of Father Stehly's first pastoral council was a source of disappointment. The council was not only the pastor's first, but the first for the parish as well. Father Stehly had expected parishioners to share his enthusiasm for it, and at the outset they did. The original pastoral councillors at St. Mary Magdalen enjoyed considerable prestige. They were proud to attend meetings, to hear the pastor's monthly reports, and to benefit from presentations by other members and invited guests. But after a while, enthusiasm began to wane. Father Stehly was disappointed as attendance dropped. Eventually he began to study the reasons why.

A common source of dissatisfaction was that councillors could not point easily to tangible accomplishments. Some complained that the pastoral council almost never reached definite conclusions. It had spent a lot of time drafting a parish mission statement, for example, and the statement did not seem to make much difference to parishioners. Another council project was about updating the concept of faith formation and boosting participation of parish families in catechesis. It was not clear to councillors, however, how they were to cooperate with the parish's faith formation office. Still other members felt that the pastor was preoccupied with a renovation of the parish's ninety-year-old church. He seemed to pay more attention to the building and fundraising efforts by the parish's Master Planning

Committee than to pastoral council issues. Whatever the truth of these complaints, Father Stehly listened.

At a council meeting on July 12, 2005, Father Stehly began to brainstorm ideas for attracting new councillors. The pastor talked about his continuing need for the pastoral council. It had already helped him with the social justice question. The council remained important, he said, even though the parish also had a Master Planning Committee. The MPC is concerned, Father Stehly said, about property use and facility renovation. The pastoral council, however, can "make sure that parishioners have a voice in planning for the parish's future." He promised that he would speak in two weeks at all of the Masses on the state of the parish. At the same time, he would invite parishioners to consider participation in the pastoral council.

At the following meeting on August 5, Father Stehly reported to the council. He described the reaction from parishioners to his "state of the parish" reflections during Masses two weeks earlier. The reactions were not as positive as he would have liked, he said, because many congregants misinterpreted his remarks. Some surmised that he simply wanted to raise money to build a new parish hall. But that was not his intention, at least not at present. Father Stehly told the councillors that he needed to lay a more comprehensive foundation for parish planning. He needed to find a way to make parishioners more realistic about the situation of the parish. The council could help, he said, by cooperating with him on a written document about the parish's future. The purpose of the document would be to help parishioners see the parish's growth and its consequences.

Also at the meeting, Father Stehly and the council developed a plan for recruiting new councillors. Central to the plan was a series of four announcements scheduled for publication in the parish bulletin in September. The announcements laid out the purpose of the council. During the next year, said the announcements, the council will focus on the changing circumstances of the parish. It will study the growth in the number of parishioners and the reduced number of priests that serve them. It will consider how the parish can maintain and expand its facilities in order to remain a center of Catholic life.

Father Stehly had reached the conclusion, in short, that he needed to be more specific about the pastoral council. By describing the council's task in specific terms—i.e., in terms of study and reflection—he was defining what would help him as pastor. He was hoping for the creation of a written document that would provide, as he said on August 5, "a more comprehensive foundation for parish planning." In addition, he was being more realistic about the kind of council members he wanted. They had to be those who could do the work of the council, the work of study and planning.

THE REPRESENTATIVE CHARACTER OF COUNCILLORS

At the July 12, 2005, meeting of the pastoral council, Father Stehly made a remark about attracting new councillors. First, he said that he was uncomfortable with open elections of pastoral council members that did not include a thorough discernment of their gifts and qualifications for the council. He had appointed the first pastoral council of twenty-two members on the basis of recommendations from parishioners. Not all of these appointed members had served in a consistent way.

Father Stehly had already made a decision that a smaller council is more manageable than the twenty-two–member council with which he had begun. He preferred a twelve-member council, a size that more closely reflects the size of councils throughout the United States.[1] Of the eight remaining council members, four had terms that were about to expire. To make up the complement of twelve members, eight new ones would have to be selected. Of these, Father Stehly wanted to be able to appoint one to ensure racial and ethnic balance. So how would the remaining seven be chosen? Some councillors had asked the pastor to consider open parish elections. Father Stehly's response reflected a common complaint about elected councils. Elected members, he said, may lack gifts and qualifications.

Councils are supposed to be representative, but in a specific way. Instead of being representative in a juridical sense, they should be a sign or witness of the entire Church.[2] They are to "make present" the wisdom of the people of God. They cannot do this if councillors lack the ability to investigate and consider, under the pastor's direction, some aspect of parish life and recommend to him their conclusions. That is what Father Stehly meant when he insisted on a thorough discernment of councillor gifts and qualifications. Good councillors must be able to carry out the council's work.

How, Father Stehly asked, can the council attract an additional seven members with the needed gifts and qualifications? Much has been written about what to look for in pastoral council members. Vatican documents have emphasized the importance of moral and personal excellence.[3] Diocesan guidelines describe the character, dispositions, and talents of the potential council member.[4] Council veterans speak of the desirable qualities and the virtues of a councillor.[5] All of these are undoubtedly important.

Among them, the most important is the ability to perform the threefold task of the pastoral councillor. It is the task of investigating and considering, under the pastor's direction, some practical aspect of ministry, and proposing its conclusions to him. Father Stehly had come to realize that the pastoral council did not exist just to represent the parish demographics. It was to help him through its efforts as a pastoral planning body. He wanted the council to help him express the needs of the parish so that parishioners could understand them. In that way they could "represent" by truly "making present" the wisdom of the community.

THE METHOD OF SELECTING COUNCILLORS

Father Stehly said that he was uncomfortable with open elections of pastoral council members, if that election did not include a thorough discernment of their gifts and qualifications for the council. So the council members developed a process of discernment. By that they meant a choice of councillors that would be reflective and well-informed. It would lead to the selection of councillors based on a thorough understanding of the council's work and of the potential councillors' personalities.

According to Benedictine Sister Mary Benet McKinney,[6] discernment occurs in four stages. It begins with the sharing of information about the council. Second, the discernment proper takes place in a series of parish meetings. Within these meetings arises the third stage. There, people are nominated, and the participants examine and weigh the nominations in dialogue. Finally, there is the act of selection, usually by ballot. The first step, the sharing of information, lays a foundation for the remaining steps. It expresses the pastor's intention, awakens the parish's interest, and builds commitment to the council. The councillors at St. Mary Magdalen Church took the work of McKinney and applied it to their own situation.

At their meeting on August 5, the council recommended a plan to select seven new councillors at an open parish meeting. At one point, the councillors had considered two open parish meetings, the first to acquaint parishioners with the pastoral council and its mission, the second to nominate and elect new members.[7] But several councillors expressed doubts. They suggested that a single meeting— to both nominate and elect councillors—might suffice if the parish were prepared in other ways. The plan was refined at the council meetings of August 31 and October 5. The preparation included four weeks of bulletin announcements. On the Sunday of the open parish meeting, a council member announced it at each Mass. Father Stehly accepted this plan.

The open parish meeting took place at the church on the evening of October 9. About seventy people attended. Father Stehly led the opening prayer and explained the process. He also expressed his hope that the council might study the needs of the parish at a time when the Catholic population is rising and the number of priests declining. The council will consider, he said, how the parish can maintain and expand its facilities and thereby remain a center of Catholic life in the city. Veteran councillors were on hand to answer questions.

Father Stehly then invited the participants to speak with the person on their right or left about the qualities they believe a good councillor ought to have. After a brief conversation, he called for silence. The pastor then led the assembly in a prayer. There was a period of further silence. After that, he called for the participants to nominate potential councillors from among their midst. Different people stood up, made a nomination, and expressed the reasons why they felt that the nominee would be a good councillor. There were eight nominees.

The nominees were then asked to state whether they accepted or declined the nomination and to give their reasons. Each spoke in turn. Some were very brief, thanking the assembly for the nomination and saying that they accepted. Some were longer. One nominee felt she had to explain why she was willing to accept nomination, even though she was a caring for a young child. Only one person declined a nomination. Father Stehly led a prayer of thanksgiving for the nominees.

He then invited the participants to come forward and to speak on behalf of the nominees, keeping in mind the tasks of the council and the nominees' qualifications. Various people came forward, briefly relating how they knew the nominees and the contributions that the council could expect from them. The meeting was supposed to end with a silent ballot. But because the council needed seven members, and a total of seven had accepted nomination, Father Stehly concluded with a prayer of thanksgiving. There was no need for a ballot. All seven were accepted, and the meeting ended with refreshments and thanksgiving.

A DISCERNING ELECTION

After the open meeting, Father Stehly and the newly chosen councillors expressed a great deal of satisfaction. One of the new councillors, Michael Brown, emphasized the importance of priests to the Catholic community. He said that they are over-extended and that he was glad to put his efforts at their service and that of the parish. Another new councillor, Agnès Chouinard, said that she looked forward to examining more closely the actual situation of St. Mary Magdalen parishioners. Good advice to the pastor, she said, depends on accurate information about the parish. Both felt that the selection process was dignified and fair.

Father Stehly was happy because the open meeting process had solved several problems. First among them was the problem of attracting councillors. He had felt, as the attendance of the twenty-two original councillors had fallen off, that people were simply not interested in the ministry. He learned that he had to become more concrete about his expectations for the council. He did not need to merely assemble "representatives" of various ministry and cultural groups for monthly discussions. Such meetings were dispiriting to the councillors, who did not see how their participation "represented" anything. The open meeting process showed the pastor that, if he were more explicit about what he expected from the council, he would attract people with that interest.

The interest that proved attractive was pastoral planning. When Father Stehly developed a more focused mission for the council, people came forward with the prospect of making a meaningful contribution and of developing concrete plans. The parishioners who attended the open meeting on October 9 knew that planning was to be the work of the council. They had an interest in the future of the parish. They could anticipate what it would take to maintain and expand the parish's capacity as a Catholic presence.

The open meeting also solved the problem of the discernment of gifts and qualifications. Father Stehly would not have welcomed an open election of pastoral council members unless it were an opportunity for discernment. The October 9 meeting provided just such an opportunity. It was a chance to share information about the council, to nominate in an open forum, to weigh the nominees, and to select them in a thoughtful way. No one at St. Mary Magdalen could complain that councillors were chosen in secret. The selection process was as open as any parish-wide election, and a lot more discerning.

NOTES

1. On the size of councils nationwide, see chap. 9 below, "Origins of the Pastoral Council," n. 20.

2. Congregation for the Clergy, *Omnes Christifideles* (Circular Letter on "Pastoral Councils"), par. 7. The concept of representation and the qualifications of councillors will be explored more deeply in chap. 9 below, "Origins of the Pastoral Council."

3. *Omnes Christifideles* speaks of councillors as "those who possess noteworthy prestige and prudence" (ibid., no. 7). Referring to diocesan councils, c. 512 §3 states that "No one except Christians of proven faith, good morals and outstanding prudence are to be appointed to the pastoral council."

4. There is a survey of what diocesan guidelines say about the qualities of councillors in Fischer, *Pastoral Councils in Today's Catholic Parish*, 63.

5. On the desirable qualities of a councillor, see Marian Schwab, "Involving the Right People: Selecting Parish Pastoral Council Members," chap. 3 in *Four Ways to Build More Effective Parish Councils: A Pastoral Approach*, ed. Mark F. Fischer and Mary Margaret Raley (Mystic, CT:

Twenty-Third Publications, 2002), 43–60, esp. 46. Schwab speaks of qualities such as spirituality, knowledge, skills, attitudes, and abilities. On the character of the councillor, see John Flaherty, "Planning: Idol or Icon of Pastoral Councils?" ibid., chap. 7, 119–136, esp. 132. Flaherty says that the good councillor should be inquisitive, unafraid of new or different concepts, able to create new ideas, practical, tolerant, and multi-disciplined.

6. Mary Benet McKinney, *Sharing Wisdom: A Process for Group Decision Making* (Allen, TX: Tabor Publishing, 1987. Reprint, Chicago: Thomas More Press, 1998). McKinney lays out the four stages of discernment on 81 and in Appendix I, 140–43.

7. The original plan for two meetings was developed after reading the article by Father Michael Parise, "Forming Your Parish Pastoral Council," *The Priest* 51:7 (July 1995): 43–47. Father Parise announced a series of three Sunday evening meetings with the explicit purpose of choosing a pastoral council. All parishioners were invited, and Father Parise sent personal invitations to a number of parishioners whom he especially wanted to consider council membership. In the meetings, he spoke in general about the purpose he envisioned for the council and put that purpose into the general context of church, discipleship, and personal formation.

CHAPTER 7

Pastoral Council Spirituality

The last five chapters have narrated stories about genuinely pastoral councils. In such councils, the pastor is the one who does the consulting. He has important questions and turns to the council for prudent answers. Councillors understand their role as serving the pastor's apostolate. By their study and reflection, they reach conclusions that will help him lead the parish effectively. The chapters suggest that authentically pastoral councils may differ from earlier pastoral councils.

> Chapter 2 told a story about Father Jim Stehly and social justice at St. Mary Magdalen Church. Father Stehly asked the council whether the parish needed to establish its own social justice committee. The council responded that parish was already active in a variety of social justice ministries, but should deepen the ministers' own self-understanding and promote their work better. Father Stehly was asking his council to study and reflect, rather than to coordinate existing ministries.
>
> Chapter 3 described the efforts at St. Julie Billiart Church to establish an outreach to Africa. When Deacon Dave Smith brought up the idea at a pastoral council meeting, Father Mike Bunny asked him to establish a committee. It explored the rationale for the African mission and recommended support for the Notre Dame Sisters' two schools in Uganda. The pastor accepted the recommendation. He had not asked the council to implement the plan, but (through the committee) to develop it.
>
> Chapter 4 depicted the effort at St. Paul of the Cross Church to build a multipurpose hall. Halfway through the fundraising part of the project, Father Patrick Gannon was told

that the parish should change direction and renovate its aging sanctuary. He consulted the pastoral council and a host of experts. The councillors agreed that a course change was possible but not advisable. Father Gannon took their advice. The parish now dedicates part of the hall rental proceeds toward the sanctuary renovation.

Chapter 5 related a conflict between the pastoral and finance councils at St. Philip's Church. A new subdivision was being built within the parish. The pastoral council anticipated greater income and was planning how to spend it. The finance council replied that it should not count its chickens until they hatched. Caught between the two, Father Leo Vicente asked each council to focus on what it did best—income estimating from the finance council, needs assessment from the pastoral council.

Chapter 6 narrated the effort at St. Mary Magdalen Church to recruit new council members. The first pastoral council numbered more than twenty. After the initial enthusiasm, absenteeism began to take a toll and attendance dropped off. Father Jim Stehly learned that, in order to renew the council, he would have to be more specific about the council's task. Only then could the parish elect members who understood the task and were committed to it.

One common feature in these brief summaries is the leadership role of the pastor. He has an agenda. He brings to the council a question. The question has practical consequences for parish ministry. The pastor invites the council to do research. He wants to plan for the future with the councillors. He is looking for thoughtful reflection, because his decisions hinge upon the answer. He has not yet made up his mind, and does not want to do so until the council has spoken. Its work will shape his apostolate.

Another common feature of the five summaries is the absence of standing committees. The pastoral council does not view itself as a "council of ministries," a body that coordinates a preexisting ministerial structure. Its members are not drawn from this ministry or that. The main work of the council is not to hear reports from the various committees or commissions. It is not a superior body that determines ministerial policies or decides questions that the subordinate groups cannot decide. No, its task is the threefold task of investigation, reflection, and the recommendation of conclusions—the task of the pastoral council that goes back to the 1965 Decree on Bishops. The five summaries above set the pastoral council apart from the so-called council of ministries.

COUNCIL SPIRITUALITY

The pastoral council idea presented in chapters 2–6 has consequences for the spirituality of pastors and councillors. Pastors consult, and to consult well requires prayerful thought. The consultative pastor not only has to define the question that he poses to the council, but has to plan the consultation. He must decide what he wants the council to study and how he wants the members to reflect on it. This entails more than drafting an agenda for a monthly meeting. It means inviting the councillors into his own apostolate. He is sharing with them his own identity and mission as parish priest.

Councillors are consultants. As members of the parish pastoral council, they are accepting an official role. They are undertaking a particular aspect of the mission of Christ, a mission defined by the Church's teaching. As councillors, they are promising to do faithfully what the Church expects of them. The Church expects them to give themselves generously to the work of investigation, reflection, and formulating conclusions. That is how, in the pastoral council, they assimilate the mission of Christ.[1]

The relationship between pastor and councillors has a spiritual dimension. The pastor consults them because he wants to exercise his office wisely and in a Christlike fashion. He believes that the Spirit of Christ dwells in his people. They too can hear and obey God's Word. In that Word the parish finds its unity. The pastor invites the councillors to enrich his understanding of his office and to shape his decisions. He hopes that they will help him discern where the Spirit of Christ is leading the parish.

Councillor–consultants freely put their gifts at the pastor's service. They recognize that the bishop has entrusted the parish to the pastor. By means of their membership in the council, they participate in the pastor's apostolate of leadership. Their job is to inquire deeply, to reflect thoroughly, and to recommend wisely. If they discharge their responsibility successfully, the pastor will accept their proposals and implement them. They will have the satisfaction of shaping his decisions. They will have contributed to his pastoral apostolate.

This description of the pastor as a consulter, and of the councillors as consultants, can lead to misunderstandings. Although the description implies that each depends on the other, some people may object to it. They may say that it gives too much responsibility to the pastor, and not enough to the council.[2] Councillors, some may say, are more than consultants. Applying the word *consultant* to councillors appears to demean them. It may suggest that their opinion is worth less than the pastor's. To speak of "consulter" and "consultants," from this point of view, impoverishes the relation between pastor and councillors.[3] It seems less collaborative and more unbalanced, as if one had all the power and the other had none.[4]

Is this a fair way to describe the pastoral council? Undoubtedly the relationship between pastor and councillors is not symmetrical. They have a consultative-only vote, and he is not obliged to accept their recommendations. On the other hand, thousands of Catholics give themselves generously to pastoral councils, believing their service to be a true experience of collaboration. In order to probe the relationship between pastors and councillors more deeply, let us revisit some of the stories from chapters 2 through 6. Our goal is to see how the relationship between the two expresses a genuinely pastoral spirituality.[5]

ENCOUNTERING CHRIST IN THE COMMUNITY

In chapter 2, we met Father Jim Stehly, the pastor who asked his council to consider whether the parish needed a social justice committee. The Archdiocese of Los Angeles had recommended social justice as a pastoral priority at the end of its 2003 synod. The synod documents had stated that every parish should establish an outreach ministry that cares for people directly or refers them to appropriate social services. Father Stehly's parish of St. Mary Magdalen did not have a social justice ministry per se. He wondered whether the parish ought to inaugurate such a ministry.

Father Stehly knew, of course, that he could simply establish such a ministry, without any consultation. Social justice is constitutive of the Church's outreach to the world, and no one would publicly oppose it. By inaugurating such a ministry, he would be responding to Cardinal Roger Mahony's request that parishes make social justice a priority. And Father Stehly knew parishioners who would willingly agree to join such a ministry. All he would need to do is put an announcement in the parish bulletin, asking for volunteers.

At the same time, Father Stehly was cautious. He remembered the opposition he had encountered when, early in his pastorate, he had made some liturgical changes. A group of parishioners at St. Mary Magdalen had not welcomed the pastor's decisions to move the U.S. flag off the main altar, to introduce new hymns, and to direct the altar servers to sit with the congregation during the Liturgy of the Word. It occurred to Father Stehly that these same parishioners might be loathe to welcome a new social justice ministry. They might take it as an implicit criticism, as if he, the pastor, had judged the parish insufficiently committed to social justice.

Father Stehly was not unwilling to exercise his leadership role. Leading the parish is part of his identity as pastor. He knew that doing social justice was more important than assuaging the delicate feelings of a few malcontented parishioners. Commitment to Christ and mission was primary.[6] At the same time, however, Father Stehly hesitated. He was still relatively new to St. Mary Magdalen. He wanted to know how the majority of parishioners, not just the malcontents, would respond to the new ministry. If only he could talk with them (he felt), he could go forward confidently.

So Father Stehly asked the pastoral council to study the matter. Although the final decision was his, he put his confidence in the councillors, most of whom were long-time parishioners.[7] He trusted in their insight. And as the council studied the matter, the members discovered twenty-one different parish organizations that were already involved in social justice ministries. Large groups like the Knights of Columbus and Catholic Charities helped the homeless, and small groups like the Sociedad Guadalupana, the parish health ministry, and the sewing circle reached out to pregnant, single women. None of these groups advertised what they did as "social justice."

The pastoral council, however, felt that it precisely described what the groups were doing. The council did not recommend the establishment of a new social justice ministry. It suggested instead that the parish should help the groups reflect on their work of justice and should promote their work. Father Stehly agreed. He was grateful to the council. The members had helped him avoid a potential embarrassment. They had shown him an aspect of what was taking place, unknown to him, right before his eyes.

The Spirit of Christ is the spirit of justice. Father Stehly, who could have inaugurated a social justice ministry without consulting anyone, turned to the pastoral council. Afterward, he felt that that Spirit had breathed through the pastoral council members. "When I had first considered the social justice ministry," Father Stehly said, "I was not thinking primarily of the sewing circle, the health ministry, and the Knights of Columbus." Revealing the social justice ministries that were already in place, Christ had spoken, Father Stehly believed, through his people.

MAKING THE CHURCH'S INTENTION OUR OWN

Sometimes pastors feel torn between their people and the hierarchical Church. The convictions of their people do not always correspond exactly to what a bishop or a Vatican document says. Ecclesiastical authority advocates one point of view, and the people advocate another. This can put a pastor in a difficult position.

In chapter 4, we met Father Patrick Gannon, the pastor of St. Paul of the Cross Church. He and his parishioners were five years along in fundraising for a new multipurpose building when they had to rethink their plans. During a visit to celebrate the sacrament of confirmation, the cardinal had indicated some displeasure with the parish's priorities. The parish did not need a multipurpose building, said the cardinal, as much as it needed to renovate its church sanctuary. Father Gannon felt awkward because he had already raised $200,000 toward the construction of the multipurpose building. He did not want to tell his people that the money would go to another project instead.

At the same time, however, the cardinal had spoken. Father Gannon could not ignore his opinion. This was more than mere politeness. When a priest is ordained, he swears obedience to the bishop and his successors.[8] By promising to obey the bishop, he dedicates himself, not to an ideal of the Church, but to the Church as it actually is. He has a relationship with the bishop that can only be called a communion.[9] It is a communion that links the priest, through previous bishops, to Christ himself. Father Gannon was not about to take the cardinal's words lightly.

Between the words of the cardinal and the pastoral council, however, there was a tension.[10] So Father Gannon renewed his consultation in earnest. His first gambit was to see whether the parish could afford to renovate the sanctuary and construct the new multipurpose building simultaneously. When that proved impossible, his second gambit was to see whether the money raised for the multipurpose building could be spent on the sanctuary renovation. The pastoral council studied the matter and concluded that it was possible but unwise. Spending the money on the sanctuary renovation may have seemed to parishioners like a bait-and-switch. The council recommended that Father Gannon hold fast to the original intention. It urged him to solicit archdiocesan permission and funds for the multipurpose building.

So Father Gannon turned to the chancery officials. To Father Gannon's surprise and pleasure, the archdiocese approved the plan. It even extended him a construction loan for $700,000. The cardinal's "course correction" turned out to be a suggestion, not a command. He was not asking for blind obedience but for serious reflection.[11] By consulting further, Father Gannon was not disobeying—he was discerning. He was genuinely weighing the prudent course. And when the process of discernment was over, and the pastor drew a conclusion different from the cardinal, the cardinal honored his decision.

Obedience to a bishop is essential to the life and ministry of a priest. Yet when tension arises between the priest's communion with his bishop and his cooperation with his people, no bishop wants blind obedience. He wants responsible discernment. This truth has consequences for the spirituality of every priest and every council.[12] Christian spirituality means assimilating the mission of Christ. Such assimilation can never be blindly obedient, mechanical, unreflective, or automatic. It demands a constant striving to make the Church's intention one's own.[13] That was the spirituality of Father Gannon and the pastoral council at St. Paul's.

THE COORDINATION OF CHARISMS

Bishops entrust parishes to pastors, and the Church uses a very traditional language to describe the pastor's work. In his leadership of the parish, the pastor is said to exercise a spiritual power[14] and even to express the authority of Christ.[15] Yet this power and authority do not exist for the sake of dominating parishioners, but rather for serving them. The priest serves by encouraging and building up the parish as the family of God.[16] In his governance of the parish, the priest helps the parish family place itself before God as an offering. Pope John Paul II said that the pastor assumes a "very delicate and complex duty" which involves "the ability to coordinate all the gifts and charisms which the Spirit inspires in the community."[17] The traditional language of parish governance is meant to express the idea of leadership. It includes the encouragement of parishioners, the recognition of their talents, and the ability to call them forth.

Father Mike Bunny, the pastor of St. Julie Billiart Church whom we met in chapter 3, provided a good example of such leadership. He had been approached by Dave Smith, the permanent deacon who is the parish's Director of Faith Formation. Smith had already developed an extraordinarily successful parish outreach to Mexico. Each spring he brought the parish's confirmation candidates south to Tijuana to build simple homes for the Mexican poor. Now Smith wanted to begin at St. Julie's an outreach to Africa. Nearby evangelical churches were dedicating a portion of their income to the African missions, and Smith believed that St. Julie's should do something similar.

Father Bunny had to calculate what this might mean. An outreach to Africa might well draw new people into parish ministry. It would certainly attract those with an understanding of the church's universal mission. But it would also require an outlay of parish money—leaving less to spend in other, equally worthy areas. Moreover, it might siphon off active parishioners from existing ministries to the new African outreach. These concerns crossed Father Bunny's mind. He had the responsibility of coordinating the parish's gifts and charisms. The development of a new ministry may well signify spiritual growth in the parish. But what will it entail? And who will exercise it?

Rather than trying to answer these questions by himself, Father Bunny asked the deacon to form a committee. This was not passing the buck. It was recognition of the talents of parishioners. They represented the communion that was St. Julie Church. By establishing a committee, Father Bunny was putting his faith in the members' ability to find a common direction.[18] He did not know whether the parish would welcome Deacon Smith's proposal. But he was confident that it should be a broader decision than the pastor's alone. To the committee he gave the spiritual and intellectual task of exploring how his suburban parish might assist the Church's outreach to Africa.

Deacon Smith had a passion for the Church's worldwide mission. He wanted to exercise that mission at St. Julie's Church. But he was not certain what form the mission should take. Defining that form occupied most of his committee's time. The members had to judge how their parish could help the Church in Africa while being a good steward of its own resources. At the end of eight meetings, the members reached a conclusion. Before establishing the committee, Dave Smith had only a vague dream of supporting Africa in general. With the committee's help, the deacon brought Father Bunny a concrete plan for supporting the Notre Dame de Namur Sisters' schools in Buseesa, Uganda.

Parish governance is the task of pastors. The Church expresses that task in the traditional terms of power and authority. But the pastor's power and authority are not like what we usually understand those words to mean. Good pastors use the power and authority of Christ to encourage, inspire, coordinate, build up, discern, and harmonize diversity. No wonder the office of pastor is a delicate and complex duty. Pope John Paul II called it an "office of love."[19] To this office, the pastoral council can make a profound contribution. Its recommendations can help the pastor make wise choices about how to exercise his own apostolate of leadership.

SHARING IN THE PASTOR'S SPIRITUALITY

Pastoral council publications commonly treat council spirituality in terms of prayer, of planning for the Church's mission, or of spiritual growth and discernment.[20] These are all essential elements in the spirituality of councils. But these publications usually do not speak of council spirituality as a share in the pastor's own spirituality. For that reason, they leave out something important. If in the pastoral council the members share in the pastor's own apostolate of parish leadership, then the spirituality of the pastor must become, to an extent, the members' own.

The spirituality of the pastor has a traditional vocabulary. It is ordinarily expressed in terms of the priest's configuration to Christ, his communion with his bishop, and his governance of the parish. This traditional vocabulary should not lead pastoral councillors, however, to conclude that priestly spirituality has nothing to do with them. They too are configured to Christ. By sharing in the pastor's work, they help him to become a true servant of the community, one who helps his parishioners realize their membership in Christ's body. Like the pastor, councillors strive to hear and obey the Word of God. They know that the parish's spiritual communion depends on it. They recognize that obedience is not a mechanism, but an act of discernment. The discernment of gifts constitutes an essential part of parish governance. The good pastor cooperates with his council in that discernment. Councillors participate in their pastor's spirituality.

Some might object to this way of characterizing the spirituality of the council. Councillors, they will say, do not merely share in the spirituality of pastors. No, they have their own spirituality, the distinctly lay spirituality of a Christian in the world. Indeed, some might argue that this is the greatest contribution that councillors can make. They broaden the pastor's understanding. They share with him the laity's point of view. They help him recall what pastors may too often forget, namely, the challenge of living as a Christian without the institutional support of Church and bishop.

This objection is somewhat plausible but ultimately unpersuasive. It reflects an outmoded interpretation of the pastoral council. According to that interpretation, councils were established so that lay people could take charge of their own parish ministries. They would do so by coordinating a system of standing committees or commissions. The pastoral council emerged at Vatican II, from this viewpoint, to promote the apostolate of laypeople. But this is demonstrably false, as we shall see in the next chapter. The pastoral council was created to aid the apostolate of pastors. To accomplish this task, councillors need to understand the pastor's work and spirituality. Only then can the pastoral council become genuinely pastoral.

NOTES

1. See Josef Sudbrack, "Spirituality (Part I: Concept)," in Karl Rahner, editor, *Sacramentum Mundi: A Concise Dictionary of Theology*, translations edited by John Cumming (New York: Seabury Press, 1975). Sudbrack defines *spirituality* as "the personal assimilation of the salvific mission of Christ by each Christian which is always in the framework of new forms of Christian conduct and is comprised within the fundamental answer of the Church to the world of salvation," 1624.

2. See chapter 11 below, "Canon 536 and Pastoral Activity."

3. Bradford E. Hinze has examined parish pastoral councils as an aspect of dialogue within the Church. He regrets the fact that pastoral councils are not required by canon law and concludes that "the consultative-only clause [c. 536] restricts collective discernment and decision making in the parish." Bradford E. Hinze, *Practices of Dialogue in the Roman Catholic Church: Aims and Obstacles, Lessons and Laments* (New York: Continuum, 2006), 37. He laments that "the consultative-only clause provides no regular means for those in authority to be held accountable for following through on the discernment and deliberation of councils or synods" (250). To be sure, there are no legal remedies for Catholics who are disappointed when their clergy fail to heed the laity's advice. Without embracing a congregational style of ecclesial polity, however, it is unclear how those without legal authority (i.e., the laity) could hold the clergy accountable.

4. William Rademacher has argued that the pastoral council's "consultative vote" reflects "the Roman, hierarchic model of church government" and that today this model "serves poorly, if at all." William J. Rademacher, "Parish Councils: Consultative Vote Only?" *Today's Parish* 32:3 (March 2000): 6–9. For a discussion of this point, see Fischer, *Pastoral Councils in Today's Catholic Parish*, 184–85.

5. The following analysis will correlate in a special way the spirituality of the consultative pastor, implicit in the Church's teaching about pastoral councils, with the traditional spirituality of the priesthood. The traditional

spirituality is reflected in Pope John Paul II, *Pastores dabo vobis* (I Will Give You Shepherds, March 25, 1992), Apostolic Exhortation following the October 1990 Synod of Bishops on the theme of "The Formation of Priests in the Circumstances of the Present Day," text and format from Libreria Editrice Vaticana (Washington, DC: United States Catholic Conference, 1997).

6. This is important for understanding the Church's teaching about how the priest is "configured" to Christ. Being rooted in Christ is the key to building communion. Such configuration is more important than loyalty to this or that segment of the Church. "Reference to the Church is therefore necessary, even if not primary, in defining the identity of the priest....Reference to Christ is thus the absolutely necessary key for understanding the reality of priesthood." John Paul II, *Pastores dabo vobis*, no. 12.

7. This reflects another aspect of the Church's teaching about how the priest is configured to Christ. He is configured in a *special* way, by holy orders, for a ministry of service (ibid., no. 12). Thus he serves his people who are configured to Christ in a *general* way. As Pope John Paul II, speaking about all Christians (and not just about priests), wrote, "The Spirit of the Son configures us in Christ Jesus and makes us sharers in his life as Son" (ibid., no. 19). To be sure, this does not deny the "specific ontological bond which unites the priesthood to Christ" (ibid., no. 18). The common priesthood of the faithful and the ministerial or hierarchical priesthood "differ essentially and not only in degree," Vatican Council II, *Lumen gentium* (Dogmatic Constitution on the Church, November 21, 1964), trans. Colman O'Neill, OP, in *Vatican Council II*, vol. 1: *The Conciliar and Post Conciliar Documents*, ed. Flannery, no. 10, 361.

8. Obedience, wrote Pope John Paul II, "is 'apostolic' in the sense that it recognizes, loves and serves the Church in her hierarchical structure....This 'submission' to those invested with ecclesial authority is in no way a kind of humiliation." John Paul II, *Pastores dabo vobis*, no. 28. It is, rather, an essential part of the priestly mission.

9. Pope John Paul II called for "a new style of pastoral life, marked by a profound communion with the pope, the bishops and other priests, and a fruitful cooperation with the lay faithful, always respecting and fostering the different roles, charisms and ministries present within the ecclesial community" (ibid., no. 18). The priest enjoys "communion" with the hierarchy and "cooperation" with the lay faithful.

10. "It is within the Church's mystery, as a mystery of Trinitarian communion in missionary tension, that every Christian identity is revealed, and likewise the specific identity of the priest and his ministry" (ibid., no. 12). Communion with the Trinity (and with the hierarchy) exists "in missionary tension." One aspect is the tension between the priest's obedience to the bishop and his sense of mission to his people.

11. The Church does not ask pastors for blind obedience: "It [obedience] flows instead from the responsible freedom of the priest who accepts not only the demands of an organized and organic ecclesial life, but also that grace of discernment and responsibility in ecclesial decisions which was assured by Jesus to his apostles and their successors for the sake of faithfully safeguarding the mystery of the Church and serving the structure of the Christian community among its common path toward salvation" (ibid., no. 28). The obedience that is necessary for ecclesial life requires "discernment and responsibility."

12. What Pope John Paul II said about the priest can also be said about the council: "The priest is chosen by Christ not as an 'object' but as a 'person.' In other words, he is not inert and passive, but rather is a 'living instrument,' as the Council states, precisely in the passage where it refers to the duty to pursue this perfection [footnote reference to the Vatican Council II document *Presbyterorum Ordinis*, 12]." Ibid., no. 25.

13. The fidelity to Christ of the priest (and, by extension, of the council) depends on a specific intention, namely, the intention of making the Church's goals one's own. "The bond with Jesus Christ assured by consecration and configuration to him in the sacrament of orders gives rise to and requires in the priest the further bond which comes from his 'intention,' that is, from a conscious and free choice to do in his ministerial activities what the Church intends to do." Ibid.

14. "By sacramental consecration the priest is configured to Jesus Christ as head and shepherd of the Church, and he is endowed with a 'spiritual power' [footnote reference to *Presbyterorum Ordinis*, nos. 2 and 12] which is a share in the authority with which Jesus Christ guides the Church through his Spirit." Ibid., no. 21. Spiritual power is not the capacity for domination but the potential for service.

15. "The priest is called to express in his life the authority and service of Jesus Christ the head and priest of the Church by encouraging and leading the ecclesial community." Ibid., no. 26. Authority is linked to the service of encouragement and leadership. The duty of the pastor to coordinate gifts and charisms is discussed by Dan R. Ebener, *Servant Leadership Models for Your Parish* (New York and Mahwah, NJ: Paulist Press, 2010). "Servant leaders empower others to reach consensus decisions, create a sense of community, are sensitive to the needs of employees, and help others to reach their full potential" (25–26).

16. The priest serves by "gathering together 'the family of God as a fellowship endowed with the spirit of unity' and by leading it 'in Christ through the Spirit to God the Father' [footnote reference to *Presbyterorum Ordinis*, no. 6]." Ibid.

17. Pope John Paul II spoke of pastoral governance as a *munus regendi*, a gift of leadership. "This *munus regendi* represents a very delicate and com-

plex duty which, in addition to the attention which must be given to a variety of persons and their vocations, also involves the ability to coordinate all the gifts and charisms which the Spirit inspires in the community, to discern them and to put them to good use for the upbuilding of the church in constant union with the bishops." Ibid. This is a part of the pastor's apostolate to which the pastoral council can make a profound contribution.

18. The priest, wrote John Paul II, "is a *servant of the Church as communion* because—in union with the bishop and closely related to the presbyterate—he builds up the unity of the Church community in the harmony of diverse vocations, charisms and services," ibid., no. 16. The unity or spiritual communion of Church members is as important as the Church's sacramental and apostolic dimension.

19. "With pastoral charity, which distinguishes the exercise of the priestly ministry as an *amoris officium*, 'the priest, who welcomes the call to ministry, is in a position to make this a loving choice, as a result of which the Church and souls become his first interest, and with this concrete spirituality he becomes capable of loving the universal Church and that part of it entrusted to him with the deep love of a husband for his wife,'" ibid., 23. The term *amoris officius* comes from St. Augustine, *In Iohannis Evangelium Tractatus* 123.5 as quoted in the *Corpus Christianorum Latinorum*, vol. 36, 678. Pope John Paul was quoting from an address to priests taking part in an assembly organized by the Italian episcopal conference on Nov. 4, 1980, published in *Insegnamenti* III/2 (1980), 1055.

20. On the council's prayer, see Kathleen Turley, "The Parish Pastoral Council and Prayer," in Arthur X. Deegan, II, Editor, *Developing a Vibrant Parish Pastoral Council* (New York and Mahwah: Paulist Press, 1995), 100–106. On planning for the Church's mission, see Marie Kevin Tighe, "Council Spirituality: Foundation for Mission," in Deegan, 88–99. On growth and discernment, see Loughlan Sofield, "A Spirituality for Councils," in Mark F. Fischer and Mary Margaret Raley, Editors, *Four Ways to Build More Effective Parish Councils: A Pastoral Approach* (Mystic, CT: Twenty-Third Publications, 2002), 23–39.

CHAPTER 8

How "Pastoral" Are Councils?

In chapters 2–7, we looked at actual pastoral councils. We saw what councils do, how they establish committees, how they differ from the parish staff, how they cooperate with the finance council, and how they select members. These chapters depicted the pastoral council idea in action.

With this chapter we begin the second part of the book. In this part we will present the pastoral idea as expressed in the documents of the Catholic Church. We will see how the Church envisions priests and bishops consulting pastoral councils to plan for the future and to solve problems by general discussion.

Pastoral councils were first recommended at Vatican II. There, in the Decree on Bishops, we read about councils consisting of representative Catholics—mainly laypersons, but occasionally priests and religious—with whom pastors meet to achieve a threefold purpose:

1. To investigate the pastoral reality;

2. To reflect on what has been learned;

3. To recommend sound conclusions.

This threefold purpose is not only the earliest and clearest description of the pastoral council. It is also the best.[1] Investigating, reflecting, and recommending, the council does pastoral planning.[2] It helps a pastor understand some aspect of the church situation and respond to it. Planning is shorthand for the threefold purpose of the council as expressed in Vatican II's Decree on Bishops.

Not everyone agrees, however, that assisting the pastor in planning is the primary purpose of these councils. Some commentators, for example, say that the parish pastoral council is a "leadership body." It leads (they say) by discerning what choices the parish ought to make.[3] Others obscure or relativize the pastoral planning role of councils by assigning to them additional tasks. These may include, for example, the work of coordinating parish ministries.[4] *Coordinating* is an ambiguous term, however, and can be taken to mean that the council directs the ministries. When councils have the task of coordinating ministries, the planning function gets short shrift.

The confusion that can arise over the primary role of the pastoral council (i.e., planning with the pastor) and its secondary roles prompts some fundamental questions:

> How do pastoral councils in the United States understand the word *pastoral*?
>
> Do pastors consult councils in order to achieve the purposes of investigating, reflecting upon, and reaching conclusions about the pastoral situation?
>
> Do pastors and councillors regard the council's work as pastoral planning?

These are the questions of this chapter. In order to answer them, we begin with a basic assumption. We assume that the pastoral council is a representative body of Catholics that the pastor consults in order to plan for the future in the threefold manner described in Vatican II's Decree on Bishops. Now we have to test that assumption. We have to discover whether pastoral councils do regard themselves and do indeed function in that way, i.e., as pastoral planning bodies.

ARE PASTORAL COUNCILS TRULY PASTORAL?

This question is difficult due to the sheer number of councils. According to *The Official Catholic Directory*, there are 18,992 parishes in the United States.[5] The *Directory* does not record how many of these parishes have a pastoral council, but one can conservatively say that they exist in three-quarters of U.S. parishes.[6] That conservative estimate is now twenty years old. More recent studies have estimated that 82 or even 90 percent of Catholic parishes have pastoral councils.[7] But even with the conservative estimate of 75 percent, we are considering 14,244 pastoral councils. That is a large number, and it is hard to say how many of, and in what sense, these councils consider themselves "pastoral."

One can hazard a guess, however, by analyzing what church guidelines say about councils. Most of the 33 archdioceses and 149 dioceses in the United States publish guidelines for councils, which include local legislation and recommendations about how best to consult them.[8] An analysis of such guidelines yields a limited but telling result. The result is limited because the guidelines do not say what councils actually do. Rather, they state what diocesan officials believe that councils should do. But given this limitation, a survey of the guidelines indicates the breadth of opinion about councils. Analysis can show the areas of agreement and disagreement. A survey of council guidelines does not reveal what actual councils do, but it does suggest the variety of opinion about them and areas of consensus.[9]

To answer the question about whether and in what sense councils think of themselves as "pastoral," I selected thirteen recent guidelines, published between 2000 and 2007. One was chosen from each of the thirteen regions into which the bishops have divided the Catholic Church in the United States.[10] The guidelines are published by the archdioceses and dioceses of Norwich, Rochester, Scranton, Charlotte, Nashville, Youngstown, Rockford, Fargo, Des Moines, Gaylord, Sacramento, Anchorage, and Pueblo. Together they constitute a sampler of guidelines for pastoral councils from around the country.

A glance at these guidelines shows that almost all assign to councils a planning role.[11] Pastors invite their councils to study and consider some aspect of church life, and the councils conclude their work by recommending a plan of action. Some guidelines describe pastoral planning at considerable length.[12] Some, using the specific language of the Church, state that councils have the threefold role of investigating, reflecting, and recommending conclusions.[13] All of this may suggest that councils widely understand their role as pastoral planning, defined in the threefold terminology that goes back to Vatican II's Decree on Bishops. It would seem that parish councils in the United States regard themselves as pastoral planning bodies. They appear to be "pastoral" councils in the specific threefold sense that this term is used in the 1965 Decree on Bishops.

A closer analysis of council guidelines, however, tempers that assertion and even puts it in doubt. The problem is not that guidelines deny to councils the planning role. No, *the problem is rather that they add duties to that role, duties above and beyond pastoral planning.* These additional duties compete with planning and may even prevent councils from accomplishing it. Several guidelines, for example, assign to pastoral councils specific administrative responsibilities. In these guidelines, as we shall see, pastoral councils have the task of implementing pastoral policies through a system of standing committees or commissions. The councils not only recommend to the pastor a plan for the future. They also implement the plan and direct parish volunteers. These additional tasks may distract attention from the council's proper role as a pastoral planner. They may even confuse parishioners as to whether volunteers are accountable to the pastor or to the council. To learn more, read on.

PLANNING *AND* IMPLEMENTING?

Let us consider, for a moment, whether the pastoral council can both plan and implement its plans. To this question, several guidelines give an unambiguous no. Some clearly state that implementation is the responsibility of the pastor and the parish staff, not the pastoral council.[14] Pastors and administrators may consult the council about how to implement parish policy, but they do not surrender to the council responsibility for implementing it.[15] In these guidelines we find a clear distinction between planning and implementing. They preserve the proper and distinctive planning role of the council, and warn against mixing it with the role of implementation.

Other guidelines, however, blend the two roles. The council plans, according to this second viewpoint, and then in addition coordinates or facilitates the implementation of its plan.[16] It implements the plan by helping parish standing committees to achieve it.[17] The council establishes goals, and the committees reach them. The council may not necessarily be the supervisor of committees, but implementation clearly belongs to its portfolio.[18] Planning and implementation by the same pastoral council, in these guidelines, are by no means incompatible tasks. The primary role of the pastoral council may be to plan, the guidelines suggest, but it has a secondary role as well, namely, to implement the plan.

Parishes often implement pastoral plans through a system of standing committees or commissions. That system (to which we will return in the next chapter) is not always the responsibility of the council. In some cases, the committees are independent of the council and not directly supervised by it. The committees implement parish plans (say the guidelines), but under the pastor's direction, not the council's.[19] Other guidelines put it in a considerably different way. They say that the planning role of councils is separate from the implementing role of committees or commissions.[20] The council plans, the commissions implement. Standing commissions and committees have a different task than does the council. Frequently they implement parish plans, sometimes under the supervision of the pastoral council, sometimes under that of the pastor.

When administrative responsibilities belong to the council, however, they can be quite demanding. To the primary duty of the council (pastoral planning), some guidelines add a second duty (implementation) and then a third duty (the supervision of standing committees). Presumably the goal is higher efficiency. The pastoral council that envisions the plan (guidelines imply) can best oversee its implementation.[21] Some councils take on more than an oversight role. They may even assume responsibility for coordinating the work of committees and commissions. Then parish commissions are accountable to the pastoral council.[22] The council is the central parish organization, and committees report directly to it.[23] To be sure, there may be an advantage to having the council not only plan, but also implement its plans through a system of committees coordinated by the council itself. But can a volunteer group like the parish pastoral council, a group that usually meets once a month, accomplish a second or even a third administrative task on top of pastoral planning?

Let us pause for a moment to see how far we have come. We began with the assumption that the pastoral council is "pastoral" insofar as it achieves the threefold purpose of councils envisioned in Vatican II's Decree on Bishops. That purpose is to investigate and reflect upon the parish reality and to reach conclusions about it, a purpose that can be called pastoral planning.

REVIEWING THE ACTUAL EXPERIENCE

We then posed the question, Are pastoral councils truly pastoral? In other words, do they accomplish this threefold purpose and regard it as their main task? The question is difficult to answer, given the vast number of pastoral councils in the U.S. Church. But the analysis of pastoral council guidelines published by U.S. dioceses provides a method. Such an analysis cannot tell us what actual councils do, but can reveal the attitudes toward councils taken by diocesan officials. The guidelines suggest what the officials expect of councils. Hence we can judge that pastoral councils in the United States are "pastoral" insofar as diocesan guidelines reflect an understanding of and commitment to the official threefold purpose.

From there we turned to the council guidelines themselves. Almost all of the thirteen guidelines chosen for analysis speak of the pastoral council as a planning body. Some of them describe planning at length, and five of the thirteen employ the actual definition of the pastoral council's role from Vatican II.[24] That would suggest that more than a third of councils are truly pastoral in the specific sense in which we are using that term. They aid the apostolate of the pastor by investigating, reflecting, and proposing to him their conclusions.

We found, however, that *the additional duties laid upon the pastoral council—duties in addition to pastoral planning—compete for the council's attention and may obscure its primary purpose.* The first of these duties is to implement what the council plans. Although some guidelines doubt whether councils can both plan and implement, others insist that they can. Moreover, some guidelines assign to the council a second task, that of coordinating a system of standing committees. They assign this task precisely to bring the council's plans to fruition. One can only wonder how successful these councils are in accomplishing the tasks of implementation and the supervision of committees in addition to pastoral planning.

More to the point, *one must ask whether a council that shoulders these administrative functions can be called truly pastoral.* In councils with such a heavy administrative load, the work of pastoral planning has to compete for the council's attention with the work of implementation and supervision of committees. At least four out of thirteen guidelines say that councils implement and supervise.[25] If the task of coordinating committees to implement pastoral plans leaves a council unable to do its main work of pastoral planning, then it is not "pastoral" in the strict sense of the word.

Yet the task of coordinating committees is what many pastoral council guidelines recommend.[26] Why do they add this administrative burden to the pastoral council, whose main task is planning? And why are we so adamant in our assumption that the planning function is primary? To answer these questions, let us turn to the documents of Vatican II, where councils began.

NOTES

1. Vatican Council II, *Christus Dominus* (Decree on the Pastoral Office of Bishops), in *Vatican Council II*, ed. Austin Flannery, vol. 1: *The Conciliar and Post-Conciliar Documents*, 564–590. See par. 27: "It will be the function of this [pastoral] council to investigate and consider matters relating to pastoral activity and to formulate practical conclusions concerning them," 580.

2. After summarizing the threefold task of the pastoral council as expressed in the Decree on Bishops (no. 27), William L. Pickett states, "The central work of a pastoral council is pastoral planning." William L. Pickett, *A Concise Guide to Pastoral Planning* (Notre Dame, IN: Ave Maria Press, 2007), 31. This assertion has been questioned by Brenda L. Hermann and James T. Gaston, *Build a Life-Giving Parish: The Gift of Counsel in the Modern World* (Ligouri, MO: Ligouri Publications, 2010). "We no longer view pastoral councils as the primary planning body in a parish," wrote Msgr. Gaston. "Planning is not an essential council function; it can be delegated to another parish group" (102–3). Why the abandonment of pastoral planning? Sr. Brenda Hermann described "the utter frustration of some pastors about the 'nitpicking' (their words) that occurred around decisions where laity's counsel was offered but was really not required" (100).

3. Jane Ferguson, *A Handbook for Parish Pastoral Councils* (Dublin: Columba, 2005), 21. Ferguson says that councillors exercise "leadership" when "they discern what is best for the parish." See also Mary Ann Gubish and Susan Jenny, SC, with Arlene McGannon, *Revisioning the Parish Pastoral Council: A Workbook* (New York and Mahwah: Paulist Press, 2001), 8. The authors say that the council is a "leadership body" whose job is to "discern and articulate the mission of the parish."

4. Sweetser and Holden, 126. The authors state that the PPC "will coordinate and give direction to all the pastoral activities and ministries of the parish" by accomplishing 13 goals (124–5), only three of which are explicitly about pastoral planning. Another example of this viewpoint is Rademacher with Rogers, 23. The authors state that the parish council "plans and coordinates the overall policy of the parish."

5. *The Official Catholic Directory* (Providence, NJ: P. J. Kenedy and Sons, 2006), "2006 General Summary," 2003.

6. The statement that 75 percent of U.S. parishes have councils is the conservative estimate of David C. Leege, "Parish Life Among the Leaders," Report No. 9 of the *Notre Dame Study of Catholic Parish Life*, edited by David C. Leege and Joseph Gremillion (Notre Dame, IN: University of Notre Dame, 1986), 6. The report's findings were also published as Jim Castelli and Joseph Gremillion, *The Emerging Parish: The Notre Dame Study of Catholic Life Since Vatican II* (San Francisco: Harper & Row, 1987), 61.

7. A more recent study states that 82 percent of Catholic parishes have pastoral councils. See Bryan T. Froehle and Mary L. Gautier, *National Parish Inventory Project Report* (Washington, DC: Center for Applied Research in the Apostolate, Georgetown University, October, 1999). The 1999 report first put the figure at 90 percent (22). Data from the newest wave of the Inventory (based on preliminary results from 8,942 parishes and reported by Froehle and Gautier at the April 2–5, 2000 annual convention of the Conference for Pastoral Planning and Council Development in Orlando, FL) suggest that 82 percent of parishes have a pastoral council, for a total of 15,728 councils. The most recent study of parish pastoral councils, based on a 2007 survey of 661 parishes, found that 93 percent have a pastoral council. See Charles E. Zech, Mary L. Gautier, Robert J. Miller, and Mary E. Bendyna, RSM, *Best Practices of Catholic Pastoral and Finance Councils* (Huntington, IN: Our Sunday Visitor Publishing Division, 2010), p. 50.

8. Mark F. Fischer, "Parish Pastoral Councils: How Many Are There? How Do Bishops Support Them?" in Ruth T. Doyle, Robert E. Schmitz, and Mary Beth Celio, editors, *Laity, Parish and Ministry*, Monograph 1 of Research Monographs of the Catholic Research Forum (Archdiocese of New York: Office of Pastoral Research and Planning, 1998), 82–106.

9. For a 1990 survey of council guidelines published by the archdioceses and dioceses of Boston, New York, Harrisburg, Raleigh, Louisville, Cleveland, Milwaukee, Fargo, Omaha, Brownsville, San Bernardino, Portland, and Cheyenne, see Mark F. Fischer, "Parish Pastoral Councils: Purpose, Consultation, Leadership," *Center Papers* no. 4 (New York: The National Pastoral Life Center, 1990). In 1995, the author completed a similar survey of the guidelines of Hartford, Ogdensburg, Philadelphia, Baltimore, Nashville, Detroit, Green Bay, Bismarck, Salina, Fort Worth, Sacramento, Seattle, and Denver. See Fischer, *Pastoral Councils in Today's Catholic Parish* (Mystic, CT: Twenty-Third Publications, 2001), 28ff.

10. The guidelines selected for the present analysis (in the order of the thirteen episcopal regions) are as follows:

1. Norwich. *Guidelines for Parish Pastoral Councils*, approved by Most.

Rev. Daniel A. Hart, March 22, 2001. Available at http://www.norwichdiocese.org/Documents.htm (accessed April 27, 2007).

2. Rochester. *Parish Pastoral Council Guidelines*, Approved by Most R. Matthew H. Clark, Bishop of Rochester, June 26, 2000. Available at http://www.dor.org/planning/Pastoral%20Council%20Development/pastoralcouncil.htm (accessed April 27, 2007).

3. Scranton. *Directives for Parish Pastoral Councils*, approved by Bishop Francis Martino, dated September 21, 2006. Available at http://www.dioceseofscranton.org/Parish%20Councils/Bishop'sLetterOnParishCouncils.asp (accessed April 27, 2007).

4. Charlotte. Bishop Peter Jugis, Diocese of Charlotte, "Guiding the Roles of Pastors and Pastoral Councils," including Appendix A: "Ministerial Responsibilities of the Commissions" (511–514) and Appendix B: "Suggested Bylaws for Pastoral Councils" (514–516), *Origins* 37:32 (January 24, 2008): 505–516. Also available at: http://www.charlottediocese.org/customers/101092709242178/filemanager/george/Pastoral_Council_Handbook_Rev_2007_Final.pdf (accessed February 13, 2009).

5. Nashville. *Parish Pastoral Council Handbook*, prepared by Ministry Formation Services (Joceline Lemaire), approved by Most. Rev. Edward U. Kmiec, January 1, 2004. Available at http://www.dioceseofnashville.com/parishpastcouncil.htm (accessed April 27, 2007).

6. Youngstown. *A Guide for Parish Pastoral Councils: A People of Mission and Vision*, copyright 2000. Available at http://www.doy.org/parish2000.PDF (accessed April 27, 2007).

7. Rockford. *Guidelines for Parish Pastoral Councils*, September 23, 1999. Available at http://www.rockforddiocese.org/planning/ PDF/PastoralCouncilNorms.pdf (accessed February 6, 2007).

8. Fargo. *Diocesan Pastoral Council Handbook* (including maps dated June 30, 2005). Very Rev. Brian Moen, Chancellor, e-mail to author, January 29, 2007.

9. Des Moines. *Pastoral Councils* (2001). The ad hoc Pastoral Council Planning Committee that formed the original document included: Mrs. Candy Chambers, Rev. David Fleming, Dr. Luvern Gubbels, Rev. Wayne Gubbels, Mrs. Cindee Hays, Rev. Gene Koch, Mrs. Shirley Koeppel, and Rev. Paul Monahan. The introduction stated that "This final document has been accepted for implementation by Bishop [Joseph L.] Charron for the formation of the Diocese of Des Moines Pastoral Council. Over time, these new Pastoral Council Principles and Guidelines will direct the restoration and/or renewal of both diocesan and parish pastoral councils" (1). Available at http://www.dmdiocese.org/files/documents/422_pastoral%20

council%20guidelines.pdf (accessed February 5, 2009).
10. Gaylord. *Parish Pastoral/Finance Council Guidelines*, approved by Bishop Patrick R. Cooney, revised November 2005. Available at http://www.dioceseofgaylord.org/inside/parish-pastoral-and-finance-council-guidelines-249/ (accessed April 27, 2007).
11. Sacramento. *Parish Pastoral Council Guidelines*, approved by Bishop William K. Weigand, November 21, 2005. Available at http://www.diocese-sacramento.org/PDFs/ParishPastoralCouncilGuidelines.pdf (accessed April 27, 2007).
12. Anchorage. *Pastoral Council Manual: A Call to Discern as Disciples* (Office of Evangelization, Archdiocese of Anchorage, approved by Most Rev. Roger L. Schwietz, OMI, June 24, 2005). Available at https://alatar.nocdirect.com/~jarchdio/documents/PastoralCouncil Manual_000.pdf (accessed February 5, 2009).
13. Pueblo. *A Handbook for Parish Pastoral Councils*. Available at http://www.dioceseofpueblo.com/Docs/Handbook%20for%20Paris h%20Pastoral%20Councils.pdf (accessed April 27, 2007).

11. The exception is the Diocese of Fargo's *Diocesan Pastoral Council Handbook*. It does not use the term *pastoral planning,* but cites c. 511, which says that the council is to "study and weigh those matters which concern the pastoral works in the diocese, and to propose practical conclusions concerning them" (quoted on 1). This description of the council's role (almost identical to that of the Vatican II Decree on Bishops, par. 27) is synonymous with pastoral planning. The Fargo handbook is an exception in the present survey because it is a handbook for the diocesan pastoral council, not for parish pastoral councils. We include it because it states that the parish pastoral council "assists the local pastor in ways similar" to the diocesan pastoral council (Glossary, a).

12. See the guidelines for Nashville (6 ff.), Charlotte (509), Gaylord (20), and Anchorage (5). One can see the same thing in the draft *Manual for Parish Councils* (draft of April 3, 2007) by the Archdiocese of Dubuque, which includes a three-page "Annual Planning Process" (4–6). Earlier guidelines of the Diocese of Charlotte treated planning in more explicit terms. See Charlotte's 1999 *Parish Pastoral Council and Commissions Manual,* 3–4, 11–13, prepared by the Office of Planning for Most. Rev. William G. Curlin (dated December 8, 1999). Downloaded from http://www.charlottediocese.org/parish.html (accessed April 27, 2007). The Charlotte manual was completely revised in 2007.

13. Some guidelines (Youngstown, 2; Rockford, 4) quote the three-fold purpose of councils from Pope Paul VI's 1966 Apostolic Letter on the Implementation of the Vatican II Decree on Bishops entitled *Ecclesiae Sanctae I* (pars. 15–16), in *Vatican Council II,* ed. Austin Flannery, vol. 1:

The Conciliar and Post-Conciliar Documents, 600–601.

Other guidelines (Fargo, 1) quote the threefold purpose from canon 511 (about *diocesan* pastoral councils). The same is apparent in the draft *Manual* from Dubuque, (3). One guideline attributes the threefold purpose (as defined in the Decree on Bishops, no. 27) to pastoral councils without citing any Vatican document (Sacramento, 2).

14. "The pastor and the parish staff members are primarily responsible for the implementation of policy in the administration of the parish" (Norwich, 2). "Pastoral councils do not implement the policy set [by the pastor], nor do they engage in the administration of the parish" (Gaylord, 15). The pastor "coordinates the implementation" (Des Moines, 5). The pastor is "responsible for leading the parish in the implementing of the plan…through the parish pastoral staff, parish organizations and/or other persons designated" (Anchorage, 5).

15. The Nashville guidelines distinguish between strategic planning (which councils do) and administrative planning (the work of the pastor, the staff, and parish organizations or committees). Nashville pastoral councils do not even tackle the more hands-on administrative planning (Nashville, 7).

16. According to the Youngstown guidelines (7), the council not only establishes a plan, but "then implements the parish pastoral plan through the coordination of various parish activities and committees."

17. In Dubuque's "draft" guidelines of April 3, 2007, the pastoral council "ratifies all the objectives for the coming year" and "the council facilitates their implementation" through standing committees or parish organizations (6). To be sure, the pastoral council does its work of implementation "by engaging in pastoral planning" (8); administration "belongs more properly to the parish staff" (35). Nevertheless the council has an administrative role. It facilitates the implementation of goals, not by means of "a controlling supervision," but through "a process for mentoring" (6).

18. In the Pueblo guidelines, "the pastoral staff assists the pastor in implementing the parish pastoral plan and parish goals" (4). That seems to suggest that the pastoral council does not have an administrative role. But the guidelines also say that it is the pastoral council's responsibility to "implement the Diocesan Pastoral Plan" and to "Develop and/or update and implement a Parish Pastoral Plan" (6).

19. According to the Rockford guidelines (5), "The pastoral council does not coordinate parish committees in the sense of directing them." This is also the case in the Gaylord guidelines. There we read that the task of "coordinating and carrying out particular aspects of parish life" belongs to committees under the pastor and his staff (17).

20. This is the case in the guidelines of Charlotte. There we read that "The parish pastoral council is the thinking, planning, reflection group for

the parish; the commissions are made up of the people that actually help to make the plan a reality" (510). The 1999 version of the Charlotte guidelines stated that one of the duties of the pastoral council chairperson is to "Insure that qualified commission chairpersons are selected" (5). See *Parish Pastoral Council and Commissions Manual*, Prepared by the Office of Planning for Most. Rev. William G. Curlin, revised December 8, 1999. Available at http://www.charlottediocese.org/parish.html (accessed April 27, 2007).

21. This is implicit in the Nashville guidelines. There, we read that "Committees are the working bodies which enable the Parish Pastoral Council to function effectively," and the task of the committees is "to implement the vision of the councils" (22). Nashville councils oversee implementation of their pastoral plan, but do not coordinate parish committees.

22. The Worship, Education, and Christian Service commissions (according to the 1996 guidelines of Great Falls—Billings, 7) are "accountable to the Pastoral Council." See the Diocese of Great Falls—Billings, *Parish Pastoral Council Guidelines*, approved by Most. Rev. Anthony M. Milone, May 26, 1996. Available at http://www.dioceseofgfb.org/Diocesan_%20Policies/parish_pastoral_council_guidelin.htm (accessed February 2, 2007).

23. According to the Pueblo guidelines, the council "is the central organization within the parish" and "All committees report directly" to it (7).

24. One guideline uses the threefold definition of the pastoral council's task (to investigate, to consider, to draw conclusions) without attribution (Sacramento, 2). Another uses it with reference to the Decree on Bishops, par. 27 (Charlotte, 507, n. 15). Two others use the threefold definition with reference to the "Implementation" of the Decree on Bishops (Youngstown, 2; Rockford, 4) by Pope Paul VI, *Ecclesiae Sanctae I* (n. 13 above).

25. In the Charlotte guidelines, the PPC has the task of "facilitating the implementation" of the pastoral plan (508), which commissions are to "carry out" (510). In Nashville, the PPC officers "facilitate the implementation" of PPC decisions (3), and committees "implement the vision of the council" (22). In Youngstown, the PPC "implements the parish pastoral plan through the coordination of various parish activities and committees" (7). In Pueblo, the PPC is to "serve as a coordinating body for all organizations and group apostolic activities" (5).

26. Councils that coordinate standing committees or commissions may well be perceived as effective, according to Zech et al., *Best Practices*. "The evidence demonstrates that both types of pastoral councils [the 'planning' and the 'coordinating' type] are associated with effective group processes" (131). The question of effectiveness differs, however, from the question of which type corresponds more closely to the Church's vision. Zech et al. note that "PPCs in our sample were more likely to view themselves as planning councils than as coordinating councils" (51).

CHAPTER 9

Origins of the Pastoral Council

The parish pastoral council is a parish council of the "pastoral" type, that is, a council of the type first established for dioceses. Vatican II recommended that bishops establish councils "to investigate and consider matters relating to pastoral activity and to formulate practical conclusions concerning them."[1] Such councils are "highly desirable," said the Decree on Bishops, because they help the bishop exercise his role as pastor, the one who knows his flock and whose flock knows him. To know his people better, the bishop inquires after "their needs in the social circumstances in which they live."[2] He may establish a pastoral council to help reach this goal. Some years after Vatican II, the Church extended the pastoral council idea from dioceses to parishes because priest pastors have much the same need as bishops. Like bishops, priests also need to investigate and reflect on the pastoral reality, and to reach prudent conclusions about it—precisely the work of the pastoral council.

HOW THIS CONCEPT DEVELOPED

So the Vatican II Decree on Bishops, we can say, is the origin of the parish pastoral council. Although the decree did not call for such councils at the parish level, it established the "pastoral" council type. Later this type was extended from dioceses to parishes, as we shall see in chapter 10. Just like its diocesan counterpart, the parish pastoral council undertakes the threefold task of examining pastoral matters, reflecting on them, and recommending its findings to the parish priest. That is what every genuinely pastoral council does or should be doing.

Not every pastoral council, however, regards itself in this way. In fact, few seem to be aware that paragraph 27 of the Decree on Bishops is the foundation of all pastoral councils. A survey of recent diocesan guidelines for parish pastoral councils testifies to this unhappy circumstance. Of the thirteen guidelines surveyed, only one cites the Decree on Bishops.[3] To be sure, they are not completely unaware of it. Two guidelines quote the Apostolic Letter of Pope Paul VI on the implementation of the Bishops Decree.[4] This letter describes the threefold purpose of pastoral councils in the language of the decree itself. So a vague link between that decree and the parish pastoral council exists in some minds. Few people, however, make the connection.

Even the guidelines that mention the Apostolic Letter of Pope Paul VI fail to recognize the debt of pastoral councils to the Bishops Decree itself. And without the Decree on Bishops we would know almost nothing of the pastoral council.[5] Why is it neglected as the source for pastoral councils? People overlook it because it recommended pastoral councils only at the diocesan (and not the parish) level. It never mentioned "parish" pastoral councils. No one would guess, from a reading of the Bishops Decree alone, that the diocesan pastoral councils recommended in 1965 gave rise to the parish pastoral councils first recommended in 1973 and later in 1983.[6]

If Vatican II did not create the pastoral councils at the parish level, how do people commonly understand their origin? Guidelines frequently link parish pastoral councils to the Second Vatican Council, but they do so in a general way. For example, they sometimes describe pastoral councils in relation to Vatican II's teaching that the Church comprises the whole people of God, and not just its pastors. Some guidelines make a distinction between the apostolate of the pastors and that of the other faithful, but they situate that distinction within an overall appreciation for the role of laypeople. Vatican II taught, they say, that baptism obligates every Catholic to participate actively in the Church. Pastoral councils are a way to participate, and they manifest the general teaching about the people of God and the participation of the laity.[7] Few know the true history, which is that parish pastoral councils are a later development of an idea first recommended in the Bishops Decree.

The official document to which people most commonly trace the parish pastoral council is the Vatican II Decree on the Apostolate of Lay People. This is remarkable, since the Laity Decree says nothing about "pastoral" councils. But it is the one document that mentions councils (albeit of a different type) at the parish level. For that reason—however mistaken—people link the Laity Decree to the parish pastoral council. Here is the relevant text from paragraph 26 of the decree:

> In dioceses, as far as possible, councils should be set up to assist the Church's apostolic work, whether in the field of evangelization and sanctification or in the fields of charity, social relations, and the rest; the clergy and religious working with the laity in whatever way proves satisfactory. These councils can take care of the mutual coordinating of the various lay associations and undertakings, the autonomy and particular nature of each remaining untouched. Such councils should be found too, if possible, at parochial, inter-parochial, [and the] inter-diocesan level, and also on the national or international plane.[8]

The Decree on the Apostolate of Lay People recommended councils—primarily at the diocesan level, secondarily at the parish level—to aid the Church's apostolate. The word *apostolate* refers to the laity's mission in the world. It is a broad concept, comprising the Church's efforts in evangelization, sanctification, charity, social relations, "and the rest"—including the realms of education, health, and culture. The lay apostolate, in short, is not confined to parish or diocesan efforts. It is the very work of Christians in the world. But people rarely distinguish between the "pastoral" councils of the Bishops Decree and "apostolate" councils of the Laity Decree. They commonly speak of the councils recommended in Laity 26 as parish "pastoral" councils. It would be more accurate to speak of them as "lay apostolate" councils.

NEED TO NOTE THE DIFFERENCE

Because paragraph 26 of the Decree on the Apostolate of Lay People contains the only reference to parish councils in the documents of Vatican II, many Catholics took this passage as a mandate. They established councils in their parishes. Even up to the present time, Laity 26 is the passage from Vatican II most often quoted in diocesan guidelines as the source for parish pastoral councils.[9] Many popular books about pastoral councils,[10] and even some scholarly treatises,[11] refer to Laity Decree 26 as their foundation. This would be a minor historical footnote were it not for the fact that the "pastoral" and the "lay apostolate" councils have different purposes.[12]

> Pastoral councils have the threefold planning function described in the Bishops Decree (par. 27), the function of helping pastors plan for the communities.
> Lay apostolate councils have the task, according to the Laity Decree (par. 26), of assisting the mission entrusted to the laity, a mission that is broader than parish or diocesan life.

In chapter 10 we will say more about the distinction between the lay and the pastoral apostolates. For now it is enough to note that they differ. Unless we make this distinction, we cannot clearly say what parish pastoral councils are supposed to do.

A further complication of the identity of parish councils emerged in the second-to-last sentence quoted above from the Laity Decree. Speaking about "apostolate" councils, paragraph 26 said that they "can take care of the mutual coordinating of the various lay associations and undertakings, the autonomy and particular nature of each remaining untouched."[13] This is the origin, I submit, of the common belief that pastoral councils are to coordinate a system of standing committees or commissions in the parish.[14] Since the late 1960s, when parish councils began, many have established such committees or commissions. There is even a name for this structure, the so-called "council of ministries."[15] People commonly assume that coordinating a committee structure is an essential feature of the parish pastoral council.

This, however, is a false assumption. First of all, the passage about coordination stems from the Laity Decree, which pertains to apostolate, not pastoral, councils. The Bishops Decree (which introduces pastoral councils) says nothing about coordinating committees. Second, the reference is to "coordinating various lay associations and undertakings." These associations and undertakings (in Latin, *consociationum et inceptorum*), are the initiatives of the laity. They are distinct from parochial committees, which are initiatives of the parish.

Finally, we read that the apostolate council may not infringe upon the autonomy of these lay associations and undertakings. But parish committees are not autonomous in the sense of being a law unto themselves. They are committees of the parish, and thus not independent.

The passage about coordination from the Laity Decree does not refer to pastoral councils and does not refer to parish committees. That was not the intent of the bishops at Vatican II. It is simply false to say that Laity 26 describes parish *pastoral* councils.

REPRESENTATION

Another argument occasionally made in support of the pastoral council as a council of ministries is that such a council is representative. The council represents the parish in the sense that its members come from its various ministerial committees and commissions. They choose representatives who then become members of the council, the so-called council of ministries, understood as the body that coordinates those ministries.

In support of this argument, one could say that the Church has emphasized breadth of makeup in the pastoral council. Vatican II called for pastoral councils to advise bishops, councils that would not be made up only of clergy, but would include religious and lay members.[16] When the Vatican extended the pastoral council idea from dioceses to parishes, it stated that the council, while not representative in a juridical sense, should be a sign or witness of the entire Church.[17] Canon law insisted that the "entire portion" of the people of God should be reflected in the pastoral council.[18] Even the most recent Vatican document that deals with pastoral councils echoed this teaching.[19] One might conclude, if one looked at these documents superficially, that they support the idea of the pastoral council as a council of ministries.

That would be a hasty conclusion. Diocesan guidelines for parish pastoral councils do not agree about the number of councillors or how to choose them.[20] The concept of representation cannot be reduced to a method of selecting councillors.[21] The Church teaches that the pastoral council represents the people of God, but not in a juridical way. Councillors are certainly not representatives in a legislature. They do not advocate for a constituency. What then is the ecclesial meaning of representation? Some say that the pastoral council mirrors a demographic profile, reflects a range of opinions, or includes a variety of gifts.[22] But selecting a council demographically, ideologically, or charismatically will not guarantee what the Church means by representation. The Church wants pastoral councils to reflect the wisdom of the people of God. They represent in that they make that wisdom present. It is the love of God expressed in prudent decisions on behalf of the community.[23]

In short, it is a false argument to say that the pastoral council, understood as the council of ministries, is more representative than councils whose members are not drawn from ministerial committees. Representation is desirable, but only as the Church understands it. Pastoral councils represent, not by selecting members in this way or that, but by making present God's wisdom. That is the Church's concept of representation. The Vatican II Bishops Decree, with its emphasis on the pastoral council that reflects the entire people of God, expresses this more strongly than does the Laity Decree.

UNDERSTANDING THE ROLE
OF PASTORAL COUNCILS

To sum up, the proper Vatican II source for the parish pastoral council is paragraph 27 of the Bishops Decree. Council guidelines should refer to it and to the later documents which applied the pastoral council idea to the parish. Paragraph 26 of the Laity Decree (with its reference to apostolate councils) is not directly relevant to the pastoral council.

No one should regard the coordination of standing committees as constitutive of the pastoral council.[24] Its constitutive role is the threefold task of study, reflection, and recommendation, the task we commonly describe as pastoral planning.

This conclusion, however, leaves the reader with a number of questions. Yes, the Bishops Decree may be the source of the pastoral council, but paragraph 27 is brief. It does not elaborate on its recommendation of pastoral councils. Even the letter of Pope Paul VI on the implementation of the decree does not shed too much light on them. So what are the "matters relating to pastoral activity" that the pastoral council investigates, ponders, and reaches conclusions about? More important, what does the word *pastoral* mean? To answer this question, the next chapter will examine the one Vatican document completely devoted to the pastoral council, the 1973 Circular Letter to the world's bishops by the Sacred Congregation for the Clergy. It first applied the pastoral council idea to the parish.

NOTES

1. Vatican Council II, Decree on Bishops, par. 27.

2. Ibid., par. 16.

3. Charlotte, 507, n. 15. The Fargo guidelines also use the threefold description, not drawn from Bishops Decree 27, but from c. 511. See chap. 8, n. 13.

4. The guidelines of Youngstown (2) and of Rockford (4) cite the threefold definition of the pastoral council from Pope Paul VI, *Ecclesiae sanctae I*, in *Vatican Council II*, ed. Austin Flannery, vol. 1: *The Conciliar and Post-Conciliar Documents*, 591–610 (see pars. 15–16 at 600–601). The Youngstown guidelines attribute the passage to Pope Paul VI without mentioning *Ecclesiae sanctae I*.

5. There is a brief mention of the Diocesan Pastoral Council in the Vatican II *Ad Gentes Divinitus* (Decree on the Church's Missionary Activity), in *Vatican Council II*, ed. Austin Flannery, vol. 1: *The Conciliar and Post-Conciliar Documents* (813–862), at par. 30.

6. In 1973, the Congregation for the Clergy published *Omnes Christifideles*, a Circular Letter to the Bishops of the World about pastoral councils, which first mentioned pastoral councils at the parish level. In 1983, Pope John Paul II promulgated the *Code of Canon Law*, which legislated about the parish pastoral council in canon 536. These two documents will be discussed in chaps. 10 and 11.

7. For the teaching about the Church as the "people of God" (the title of chap. 2 of the *Dogmatic Constitution on the Church*), see the guidelines of Norwich, 1. The Scranton guidelines (8) distinguish between the apostolate of pastors and that of the laity (quoting The Decree on the Apostolate of Lay People, par. 10), but state that the Church needs the participation of the laity. The whole Catholic people are in the process of being conformed to Christ as priest, prophet, and king, say the 1996 guidelines of Great Falls–Billings (1, quoting the Dogmatic Constitution on the Church, pars. 10–13).

8. Vatican Council II, *Apostolicam actuositatem* (Decree on the Apostolate of Lay People), in *Vatican Council II*, ed. Austin Flannery, vol. 1: *The Conciliar and Post-Conciliar Documents*, at par. 26 (791).

9. In his January 15, 2004 prefatory letter to the Nashville guidelines, Bishop Edward Kmiec cites Laity Decree 26 (about "lay apostolate" councils) as the foundation for the parish "pastoral" council. The guidelines for Charlotte (507, n. 14), Rockford (4), and Sacramento (7) quote the same passage.

10. Among the popular books that cite par. 26 of the Laity Decree as the foundation for the parish pastoral council, see Gubish et al., 4; John Heaps, *Parish Pastoral Councils: Co-responsibility and Leadership* (Ridgefield, CT: Morehouse, 1993.), 10; and Rademacher with Rogers, 21, n. 1. The earlier popular literature is surveyed by Fischer, *Pastoral Councils in Today's Catholic Parish*, chap. 12, n. 23.

11. Among the scholarly authors who cite par. 26, see Robert J. Ahlin, "Parish Councils: A Theological and Canonical Foundation," JCD diss. (Washington, DC: The Catholic University of America, 1982), 78–9; E. Caparros, E. M. Thériault, and J. Thorn, eds., *Code of Canon Law Annotated*, Latin-English edition of the Code of Canon Law and English-language translation of the fifth Spanish-language edition of the commentary prepared under the responsibility of the Instituto Martín de Azpilcueta (Navarra), a collaboration of the Faculties of Canon Law of the University of Navarra in Spain and Saint Paul University in Canada (Montreal: Wilson and Lafleur, 1993), see the commentary on c. 536 by J. Calvo at 394; William Dalton, "Parish Councils or Parish Pastoral Councils?" *Studia canonica* 22 (1988): 169–185; Mark S. Mealey, "The Parish Pastoral Council in the United States of America: Applications of Canon 536," JCD diss. (St. Paul University, Ottawa, 1989), 163; and John A. Renken, "Pastoral Councils: Pastoral Planning and Dialogue among the People of God," *The Jurist* 53 (1993): 132–154. These are discussed in Mark F. Fischer, "What Was Vatican II's Intent Regarding Parish Councils?" *Studia canonica* 33 (1999): 5–25.

12. Peter Kim recognized this distinction and proposed that parishes establish two councils, a "pastoral" and a "coordinating" council. Peter Kim Se-Mang, *Parish Councils on Mission: Coresponsibility and Authority among Pastors and Parishioners* (Kuala Lumpur: Benih Publisher, 1991), 83.

13. Vatican Council II, *Apostolicam actuositatem* (Decree on the Apostolate of Lay People), par. 26. The word *coordinate* is not used in the final text of the Decree on Bishops to describe the "pastoral" council. At one point, however, a use of that word was contemplated. Roch Pagé relates how the Preparatory Commission known as "De Episcopis" drafted a schema entitled "De Cura Animarum" (April, 1963). The schema included a proposal for a Diocesan Pastoral Council which would (among other things) ensure the coordination of the works of the apostolate, as well as a proposal for a Diocesan Coordinating Council, which would do the actual coordinating of the apostolate itself. In the spring of 1964, the Mixed Preparatory Commission known as "De Episcopis et Religiosis" prepared a text entitled "De pastorale episcoporum munere in ecclesia." This text became the basis for the Bishops Decree. Pagé states that Bishops Decree 27 was taken "almost entirely" from the passage in "De Cura Animarum" about coordinating councils. But the final text dropped the reference to the coordination of apostolic works, Pagé continues, "chang-

ing *opera apostolatus* to *opera pastoralia*." See Roch Pagé, *The Diocesan Pastoral Council*, translated by Bernard A. Prince (Paramus, NJ: Newman Press, 1970), 20. The close connection between "pastoral" and "apostolic" councils (if not the pastoral and lay apostolates) suggests that the two functions at one time were not considered incompatible.

14. The practice of having councils coordinate standing committees may be declining. In a 1990 survey of 13 guidelines for parish councils, ten out of thirteen dioceses specified a structure of standing committees (Fischer, "Parish Pastoral Councils," table 6, 7). In a 1995 survey of thirteen other guidelines, the number dropped to eight (Fischer, *Pastoral Councils in Today's Catholic Parish*, chap. 4, n. 2). In our present study, three out of thirteen guidelines specify such a structure: seven commissions (Charlotte, 515), five committees (Pueblo, 7), or three committees or commissions (Nashville, 26–31). A three-commission structure is also recommended in the 1996 guidelines for Great Falls–Billings,(6).

Interestingly, the Youngstown guidelines offer two basic pastoral council models: one, the "council of ministries" which "coordinates" seven essential committees (7); and the other, the "pastoral planning" model, in which committees work "independently" of the pastoral council (10).

Although the Rockford guidelines state that the pastoral council "determines" the commissions or committees needed, nevertheless the council "does not coordinate parish committees in the sense of directing them" (5). In other dioceses, however, this is not the case. In Pueblo, "All committees report directly" to the pastoral council (7). Also in the guidelines for the Great Falls–Billings diocese, commissions are "accountable" to the pastoral council (7).

15. Sweetser and Holden, 126 ff.

16. *Christus Dominus* (Decree on the Pastoral Ministry of Bishops) in *Vatican Council II*, ed. Austin Flannery, vol. 1: *The Conciliar and Post-Conciliar Documents*, par. 26.

17. Congregation for the Clergy, *Omnes Christifideles* (Circular Letter on Pastoral Councils), par. 7.

18. *Code of Canon Law*. About the diocesan pastoral council, c. 512 §2 states: "The Christian faithful who are appointed to the pastoral council are to be so selected that the entire portion of the people of God which constitutes the diocese is truly reflected, with due regard for the diverse regions, social conditions and professions of the diocese as well as the role which they have in the apostolate, either as individuals or in conjunction with others."

19. Congregation for Bishops, *Apostolorum successores* (Directory on the Pastoral Ministry of Bishops), no. 184. This 2004 document shall be discussed at greater length in chap. 13 below.

20. Regarding the number of council members, the guidelines for the Diocese of Sacramento allow for the smallest council, a minimum of 6 members (and a maximum of 15). The Diocese of Norwich allows for the largest number, a maximum of 18 members (and a minimum of 7). Other ranges include 7–15 (Rochester), 8–12 (Scranton), 8–15 (Youngstown). Some do not specify a number of councillors or range of numbers (Charlotte, Nashville, Rockford, Fargo, Des Moines, Gaylord, and Pueblo). Zech, et al., state that, in 661 parishes surveyed, the average number of PPC members is 12.4 (Table 3.3, p. 56). 49 percent of councils have at least one member who is elected at large (Table 3.4, pg. 59). Election at large is the most common means of selecting council members.

21. Guidelines show that some dioceses recommend an open election (Rochester, Charlotte, Nashville), either by the parish at large or by an unspecified committee. Other dioceses recommend either election or appointment (Des Moines, Sacramento, and Pueblo). One calls for only the appointment of diocesan council members (Fargo). Gaylord recommends a "process of calling forth and biblical selection" (16), and Pueblo allows for a process of "casting lots" (10). The Youngstown guidelines specifically state that members are to be "appointed from various ministerial committees" (i.e., the "council of ministries" model, 7). The fact that only three of the guidelines surveyed recommend open elections marks a shift from what was hitherto the norm. "Of the thirteen guidelines surveyed in 1995, nine recommend the election of most council members....Three others allow the selection of councillors by drawing lots as an alternative to parish-wide elections....One guideline allows for election of members by the pastoral council itself or by ministerial committees as an alternative to parish-wide elections" (Fischer, *Pastoral Councils in Today's Catholic Parish*, chap. 7, n. 3).

22. One survey of diocesan guidelines for pastoral council showed that, in most cases, representation is a demographic concept. One calls for the appointment of members to achieve a balance of knowledge and competence. Others call for representation in the sense of making present the concerns and needs of various groups, or manifesting different attitudes. See Fischer, *Pastoral Councils in Today's Catholic Parish*, 62–63.

23. Ibid., 149.

24. Gubish, et al., rightly observe (10) that the movement from "the current parish council model" (i.e., away from the "apostolate" council of par. 26 in the Laity Decree) to the parish pastoral council is a movement away from coordinating ministries. By referring to the PPC as a "leadership body" (8), however, Gubish et al. may blur the distinction between the pastor (to whom the bishop entrusts the parish) and the consultants upon whom the pastor relies.

CHAPTER 10

What *Pastoral* Means

Bishops entrust parishes to pastors because they have confidence in their character and ability. The good pastor is the one who strives to know his people and serve them. He takes seriously the words of Jesus, "I am the good shepherd." Like Jesus, a good pastor can say, "I know my own and my own know me" (John 10:14). This is one reason why he consults his pastoral council. He wants to benefit from the members' knowledge of God and of one another. They in turn want to participate in the local Catholic community for whom he serves as pastor.

By asking councillors to study an aspect of the pastoral situation, to consider it with him, and to recommend their conclusions, the pastor implies several things about his relation to the council. He implies, first of all, that he recognizes that his knowledge is limited. Parishes comprise many people, and the pastor cannot possibly know them all. Many issues arise of which the pastor has little experience. So he turns to knowledgeable parishioners in the hope that, through dialogue with them, he may learn more about the pastoral situation and make better decisions regarding it. Like Socrates in the dialogues of Plato, the good pastor says, "I do not think that I know what I do not know."[1] He is modest about his knowledge. He consults his people to learn more. Consultation expresses the honesty and humility of the good pastor.

Second, when the pastor consults his people, he is putting his faith in dialogue. By *dialogue* I mean a general discussion in which different views are expressed and participants learn from one another.[2] There are many kinds of truth and many ways to approach the truth of a matter. In some cases, where a question requires specialized knowledge, one has to consult experts. But in other cases, where a question requires knowledge of the community, expert opinion may not be what is needed. The truth may depend on the situation in which the community finds itself. In these kinds of cases, only a discussion with wise community members will suffice. The truth can emerge only in the give and take of conversation. When a pastor consults, he implies a belief in the value of dialogue, which holds opinions up to the light of reason informed by faith.[3]

Finally, the consultative pastor also expresses confidence in his people. By consulting them, he implies certain expectations. He expects them to perform in a thorough way the task of the council, namely, to investigate and ponder the pastoral situation and draw wise conclusions. Moreover, he expects to benefit from their work. He hopes to learn from his dialogue with them. Doubtless, he cannot ask councillors to assume the role of pastor. The bishop entrusted the parish to him, and he alone is accountable for it. But when the pastor consults his councillors, he is putting his trust in them. He trusts them to broaden his understanding of the pastoral reality, a reality about which he wants to know more. He expects them to share their wisdom with him.

In short, the pastor consults in order to be a good shepherd. Council members share in his apostolate. Being responsible for study, reflection and reaching sound conclusions, they participate in the office of pastor. They may not themselves hold office in the parochial Church, but they contribute to the pastor's office. Councillors contribute to it through their work of pastoral planning. Their work is pastoral because it helps the pastor to make wise decisions on behalf of the parish. That is the key to understanding the word *pastoral*. A pastoral council strengthens the apostolate of the pastor.

THE 1973 CIRCULAR LETTER

This understanding of the word *pastoral* became explicit in the 1973 Circular Letter to the bishops of the world from the Vatican's Sacred Congregation for the Clergy. Entitled *Omnes Christifideles*, the Circular Letter is the only Vatican document entirely devoted to pastoral councils.[4] It is also the first document to extend the concept of the pastoral council from dioceses to parishes. Anyone who wants to know the Church's teaching about pastoral councils must consult *Omnes Christifideles*.[5]

The letter begins with an acknowledgement that all Christians belong to the priesthood of the faithful. In terms of this priesthood, they have a mission or apostolate. It is to express their faith in their daily lives. The apostolate of the laity, states *Omnes Christifideles*, is the "sanctification of the world" (par. 1). In other words, all Christians have a mission to help establish God's kingdom by discharging their everyday responsibilities. The laity's mission is more general than the mission of pastors.

The pastors' mission, by contrast, is the work of leading a congregation. *Omnes Christifideles* calls it the task of "teaching, sanctifying, and ruling" (par. 3). Pastors exercise this responsibility in what the letter calls an "immediate" way. This means that pastors need not seek the permission of parishioners, including the pastoral council, before doing their work. Laypeople can assist, however, in the mission of the pastor. Indeed, *Omnes Christifideles* states that concern for the gospel may even oblige them to lend their assistance.[6] They can do so in a variety of ways, and the pastoral council is one of them. When pastoral council members do their work of pastoral planning, they are cooperating in the pastor's apostolate.[7]

People frequently misunderstand the pastoral council, however, as an expression of the apostolate of the laity. For every pastoral council guideline that correctly identifies such pastoral councils as a contribution to the apostolate of the pastor,[8] there are three that quote the Decree on the Apostolate of Lay People and portray the pastoral council as an expression of the lay apostolate.[9] Other guidelines for pastoral councils refer to the Dogmatic Constitution on the Church as a source.[10] They cite its references to the baptism of the faithful and the people of God, as if pastoral councils were meant to enable laypeople to exercise their vocation in the world. This is inaccurate. The pastoral council assists the pastor in exercising his own office of community leadership.

POPULAR MISCONCEPTIONS

Omnes Christifideles clearly taught in 1973 that the pastoral council is an instrument of the pastor's apostolate. For that reason we call the council "pastoral." However, diocesan guidelines for councils rarely cite this letter. Because the letter is so little known, various misunderstandings of the term *pastoral* have arisen. One misunderstanding is that pastoral refers to a kind of prayerful spirituality. This view goes back at least to 1985 and an influential manual for parish councils published by the Archdiocese of Milwaukee. The manual listed seven essential characteristics of the parish council, the first of which was that the council is prayerful.[11] This list of seven characteristics has been frequently reprinted in secular publications about councils as well as in diocesan guidelines.[12] Many publications not only say that prayer is essential to the pastoral council but also publish prayers that councils can use.[13] One diocesan guideline even goes so far as to specify how much time a council should spend on prayer.[14]

An emphasis on prayer is holy and good, but it is not the defining characteristic of the parish pastoral council. Prayer is no more essential to the pastoral council than it is, for example, to the Legion of Mary, the liturgy committee, or to meetings of the St. Vincent de Paul Society. Each of them affirms the words of St. Paul: "Rejoice always, pray without ceasing, give thanks in all circumstances" (1 Thess 5:16–17). This is no truer for the pastoral council than it is for any other Christian group. Pastoral refers to the council's participation in the office of the pastor, not to how much time it spends in prayer.

Another misconception about the meaning of *pastoral* is that it refers to a style of decision-making. The pastoral council, according to this viewpoint, avoids parliamentary procedure and engages in spiritual discernment and the search for consensus. A discerning style, along with being prayerful, is one of the Milwaukee Archdiocese's seven essential characteristics of the parish council. The council is pastoral, according to this viewpoint, precisely because it discerns when it makes decisions.[15] Although some council guidelines allow the use of parliamentary procedure, such as *Robert's Rules of Order*,[16] others state that a discerning search for consensus is preferable, especially when council recommendations have important consequences for the parish. One guideline even states that consensus "has been shown to be the most Christian manner of problem-solving."[17]

The search for consensus and the use of a discerning style, however, are not what define the pastoral council. A council is not more pastoral if it avoids parliamentary procedure. Indeed, some leaders in the pastoral council movement have shown how valuable such procedures can be.[18] Spiritual discernment and the search for consensus are not incompatible with a careful use of *Robert's Rules of Order*. Problems can arise in a group whose members are unfamiliar with parliamentary procedure, however, just as they can arise in any group where some members seek an unfair advantage over others. The council is pastoral because of its relation to the pastor. Pastoral councillors should not look to a style of decision-making as the key to what *pastoral* means.

A final popular misconception is that the subject matter of "pastoral" councils is more spiritual than the subject matter of old-fashioned "parish" councils. "Parish" councils supposedly were preoccupied with parish administration, and "pastoral" councils are not. For many popular writers of the 1980s and 1990s, the word *pastoral* meant that councils follow the Holy Spirit so as to fulfill the parish's spiritual mission.[19] Councils were to help create "a vision for parish life, mission, and ministry" and to be places for "implementing spirituality."[20] In the view of many, this meant that parish administration was off limits to the pastoral council, that is, incompatible with its "pastoral" character. This misunderstanding persists today. Some guidelines for parish pastoral councils specifically forbid them from discussing administrative matters, except insofar as administration is a part of the council's work of pastoral planning.[21]

In 1973, however, *Omnes Christifideles* made it plain that the scope of the pastoral council (at the diocesan level) is very broad and not limited to a "spiritual" subject matter. The Circular Letter put it this way:

> Those questions may be committed to its [the diocesan pastoral council's] study which, whether indicated by the diocesan bishop or proposed by the council members and accepted by him, refer to pastoral care exercised within the diocese. It is, however, beyond the competence of this council to decide on general questions bearing on faith, orthodoxy, moral principles or laws of the universal Church.[22]

In short, a pastor may consult about virtually any practical aspect of pastoral care. He can propose the question, or the councillors can propose it (provided that he accepts it as a topic for consultation). The questions must be practical, that is, having to do with correct action. "General" questions about faith, morality, and Church law are excluded. But there is certainly no suggestion that the scope of the "pastoral" council is limited to a "spiritual" subject matter, and no suggestion that administrative topics are off limits. The pastoral council is pastoral, not because it has a limited scope, but because it helps the pastor make wise decisions.

BETWEEN VATICAN II AND THE 1983 CODE

Some may object to this definition of the word *pastoral* on the grounds that *Omnes Christifideles* was about *diocesan* pastoral councils, not *parish* pastoral councils. They may say correctly that Vatican II never spoke of pastoral councils at the parish level, and that the only Vatican II reference to parish councils was in the Decree on the Laity. They may accept the popular claim that a parish council is "pastoral" because it is more spiritual than temporal, more discerning than parliamentary, and more visionary than administrative. They may even affirm the belief that it expresses the lay apostolate rather than the pastor's.

The Church's official documents, however, tell a different story. The spirituality of councils is important, but it is not what makes them pastoral. Councils should be discerning, but they are not more pastoral because they embrace a certain style of decision-making. Pastoral planning is the proper role for councils, but they can plan about any practical topic, and are not less pastoral if they focus on parish administration. Councils are pastoral when their work of study, reflection, and recommendation helps the pastor to do his job better. In such councils, members share in the apostolate of pastors.[23]

Omnes Christifideles occupies an important transitional position between the documents of Vatican II and the 1983 Code of Canon Law, which first legislated about parish pastoral councils. Vatican II introduced the pastoral council only at the diocesan level, but the 1973 Circular Letter extended the concept to parishes.[24] It said, "There is nothing to prevent the institution within the diocese of councils of the same [pastoral] nature and function, whether parochial or regional as they are called (for various deaneries or social bodies, etc.)."[25] In other words, *Omnes Christifideles* made it clear that the "pastoral" council is a type of council, the type that investigates, ponders, and proposes conclusions to the pastor. The council can be found in the diocese or in the parish. Pastors, whether they are bishops or priests, may consult this council to help them exercise their office wisely. The pastoral council primarily serves the pastor's apostolate of leading the parish, not the lay apostolate of service to the world.

NOTES

1. Plato, *Apology* 21d, trans. Hugh Tredennick, in Plato, *Collected Dialogues*, edited by Edith Hamilton and Huntington Cairns, Bollingen Series LXXI (Princeton, NJ: Princeton University Press, 1963), 8. For a discussion of the role of the Platonic Socrates as a model for the consultative pastor, see Mark F. Fischer, "Parish Councils: Where Does the Pastor Fit In?" *Today's Parish* 23:7 (November/December 1991): 13–15.

2. The phrase "by general discussion" comes from the Decree on the Laity, par. 10. Pope John Paul II cited this as a source for the pastoral council. See his *"Christifideles Laici*: Apostolic Exhortation on the Laity" (January 30, 1987), based on the 1987 World Synod of Bishops, *Origins* 18:35 (Feb. 9, 1989): 561, 653–59. It stated, "The [Second Vatican] council's mention of examining and solving pastoral problems 'by general discussion' [footnote reference to Decree on the Laity, no. 10] ought to find its adequate and structured development through a more convinced, extensive and decided appreciation for 'parish pastoral councils,' on which the synod fathers have rightly insisted" (no. 27, 574).

Seven years earlier, Thomas J. Green, an American canon lawyer, referred to the Decree on the Laity, par. 10, as a source for parish councils. See Green's "Critical Reflections on the Schema on the People of God," *Studia Canonica* 14 (1980): 235–314. Green criticized the lack of attention to parish pastoral councils in the draft schema for the revised Code of Canon Law (*Studia*, p. 254). In a footnote about parish councils he wrote, "The schema does not seem to refer to corporate bodies at the parish level," adding that "The thrust of *Apostolicam actuositatem* (nos. 10, 26) and the Directory on the Pastoral Office of Bishops (no. 179) took a different view on the matter." In other words, the two documents did refer to parish councils, but the draft schema did not (and should have).

3. Pope Paul VI affirmed this understanding of dialogue in his first encyclical letter, *Ecclesiam Suam*. In a commentary appended to the letter, Gregory Baum, OSA, wrote, "By introducing the notion of dialogue (human dialogue leading men into divine dialogue), the Pope seeks...a more unified understanding of the church's mission" (11).

4. Sacred Congregation for the Clergy, *Omnes Christifideles* (Circular Letter on "Pastoral Councils"), reprinted in O'Connor, ed., *Canon Law Digest* 8, 280–288. The circular letter was also published in *Origins* 3:12 (September 15, 1973): 186–190, and is available at http://www.PastoralCouncils.com/bibliography/vatican-documents/post conciliar/circular/. The Sacred Congregation for the Clergy was established on August 15, 1967. On May 5, 1969, John J. Wright, the Bishop of Pittsburgh who had written the introduction to a 1967 book by Bernard Lyons entitled *Parish Councils*, became Prefect of the Congregation. The Circular Letter was published over Wright's name.

5. For a history of *Omnes Christifideles*, and in particular its relation to the Dutch National Pastoral Council, as well as efforts in the United States to establish a National Pastoral Council, see Fischer, *Pastoral Councils in Today's Catholic Parish*, chap. 10.

6. *Omnes Christifideles* (in par. 4) quotes the Vatican II *Lumen Gentium* (Dogmatic Constitution on the Church), in *Vatican Council II*, ed. Austin Flannery, vol. 1 *The Conciliar and Post Conciliar Documents*, at par. 37, 394.

7. *Omnes Christifideles* (in par. 4) quotes from the 1971 Synod of Bishops, *The Ministerial Priesthood* (*De Sacerdotio ministeriali*), in O'Connor, ed., *Canon Law Digest*, vol. VII, 342–366. The synod said that the pastoral council "is to offer, after study and consideration, its conclusion as to what is necessary for the diocesan community to organize the pastoral work and to execute it efficiently" (part 2, par. 11, n. 3, cited at 364).

8. The guidelines published by the Diocese of Scranton rightly say that the pastoral council represents the "collaboration of the faithful in the development of pastoral activity which is proper to priests." They quote from "The Priest, Pastor and Leader of the Parish Community," an "Instruction" from the Congregation for the Clergy (August 4, 2002), par. 26, downloaded from http://www.vatican.va/roman_curia/congregations/cclergy/documents/ rc_con_cclergy_doc_20020804_istruzione-presbitero_en.html (accessed on July 30, 2007).

9. See above, chap. 9, n. 9, for references in diocesan guidelines to the Vatican II Laity Decree. Ferguson (20, n. 3) and Gubish et al. (7, n. 5) quote the Laity Decree, paragraph 10, about laypeople as "participators in the function of Christ as priest, prophet, and king." They imply that the pastoral council has to do with the apostolate of the laity. It would be more correct to say that the pastoral council has to do with the apostolate of the pastor, the apostolate of "teaching, sanctifying, and ruling" (*Lumen Gentium* [Dogmatic Constitution on the Church], par. 32).

10. See above, chap. 9, n. 7, for references in diocesan guidelines to the Vatican II's *Lumen Gentium* (Dogmatic Constitution on the Church).

11. Archdiocese of Milwaukee, *Living the Spirit: A Parish Council Manual*, fourth edition, Denise Pheifer, ed., original copyright 1985 (Archdiocese of Milwaukee: Office for Parish Stewardship and Lay Leadership Development, 1991), 7–8. The manual states that one of the essential characteristics of a parish council is that it is "pastoral," but defines *pastoral* without reference to the pastor.

12. Rademacher with Rogers, *The New Practical Guide*, reprinted the seven essential characteristics on 24–26; so did the Diocese of Gaylord, *Guidelines*, 11.

13. For an extensive collection of council prayers, see Gubish et al., *Revisioning*, 17–54; and also the Diocese of Charlotte's 1999 *Manual*, 17–21.

14. "To insure the proper role of discernment in the apostolate of the Parish Pastoral Council, each meeting is to begin with a period of prayer for twenty minutes." Diocese of Scranton, *Directives*, 13.

15. For "discerning" as one of the seven essential characteristics, see the Milwaukee Archdiocese's *Living the Spirit*, 7–8. Gubish et al. state that the pastoral council evolved from "business and politics" toward "prayer and discernment," 10.

16. Henry M. Robert, *Robert's Rules of Order Revised* (Chicago: Scott Foresman and Company, 1990).

17. Guidelines that allow the use of parliamentary procedure include Gaylord, 14 (which nevertheless encourages consensus, 3). Others reject the use of parliamentary procedure (Scranton, 13) and encourage consensus techniques (Anchorage, 3), because "Voting sets up a win/lose situation" (Norwich, 2). The quote about consensus being the most Christian manner of problem-solving is from the Diocese of Pueblo, 8.

18. An argument for parliamentary procedure as the normal way of making decisions is advanced by Robert G. Howes in his books, *Creating an Effective Parish Pastoral Council* (Collegeville, MN: Liturgical Press, 1991), 50, and *Parish Planning: A Practical Guide to Shared Responsibility* (Collegeville, MN: Liturgical Press, 1994), 144–47. The dangers to effective ministry from a time-consuming search for consensus are outlined by Loughlan Sofield, Rosine Hammett and Carroll Juliano, *Building Community: Christian, Caring, Vital* (Notre Dame, IN: Ave Maria Press, 1998), 113.

19. One reads, for example, that the pastoral council "strives to discern the movement of the Holy Spirit" so as to help the parish "perform its *spiritual* mission." Rademacher with Rogers, 24.

20. On the "vision," see Enda Lyons, *Partnership in Parish: A Vision for Parish Life, Mission, and Ministry* (Dublin: Columba, 1987). On "spirituality," see David L. Vaughn, "Implementing Spirituality in Catholic Parish Councils," thesis submitted in partial fulfillment of the requirements for certification in the National Association of Church Business Administration at

the University of St. Thomas (St. Paul, MN: University of St. Thomas, 1994). A focus on vision, however, can lead to vagueness. One pastoral council guideline from the 1980s (now superseded) stated that councils have the task of creating parish policy, defined as "somewhat vague, idealistic hopes." See the pastoral council guidelines of the Diocese of St. Augustine, Florida, entitled "Ten Guiding Principles of Parish Councils," written by Msgr. Joseph Champlin in consultation with the presbyteral council (St. Augustine, FL: Office of the Chancery, 1985), in principle eight.

21. "The council focuses on anything except administration, faith, orthodoxy, moral principles or laws of the universal Church" (Diocese of Rockford, 9). Rockford added the word *administration* to the other four, which were taken from *Omnes Christifideles*, par. 9 (see n. 22, below). The Diocese of Sacramento eliminates from the scope of pastoral councils "acts of administration which are distinct from pastoral policies and planning" (5). By contrast, the Pueblo guidelines rightly say that the pastoral council may advise about "all matters of the parish except where specifically limited by Church laws, diocesan policy or the documents of the Second Vatican Council" (3). Some popular authors also exclude administration. Ferguson states, "The Parish Pastoral Council is concerned with issues that affect the lives of parishioners rather than the administration or financial management of the parish" (52).

22. Congregation for the Clergy, *Omnes Christifideles*, par. 9.

23. Hans Küng, "Participation of the Laity in Church Leadership and Church Elections," trans. by Arlene Swidler, *Journal of Ecumenical Studies* 6:4 (Fall 1969): 511–533. As early as this publication, Küng saw (528) a parallel between diocesan pastoral councils and the kind of parish councils that could develop along "pastoral" lines.

24. This was brought to my attention by Renken, "Pastoral Councils: Pastoral Planning and Dialogue," 138.

25. Ibid., par. 12.

CHAPTER 11

Canon 536 and Pastoral Activity

Pastoral councils got their start, at least at the diocesan level, through the documents of Vatican II. Eight years later, in 1973, the Circular Letter to the world's bishops from the Sacred Congregation for the Clergy said that pastoral councils could be established in parishes. Ten years after that, the first legislation about such councils appeared.

In 1983 Pope John Paul II promulgated a new Code of Canon Law. The code included a single canon about the parish pastoral council. Canon 536 has two paragraphs:

> §1. If the diocesan bishop judges it opportune after he has heard the presbyteral council, a pastoral council is to be established in each parish, over which the pastor presides and in which the Christian faithful, together with those who share in pastoral care by virtue of their office in the parish, assist in fostering pastoral activity.

> §2. A pastoral council possesses a consultative vote only and is governed by the norms established by the diocesan bishop.[1]

Canon 536 was decisive. Henceforth the parish council would be the parish "pastoral" council. This is the type of council first described in the Vatican II Decree on Bishops, the type with a three-fold task of investigating and pondering matters and formulating practical conclusions. But canon 536 does not mention Vatican II's threefold description of the pastoral council task. What is the relation between canon 536 and paragraph 27 of the Bishops Decree? That is the topic of this chapter.

The canon makes remarks about council leadership, membership, and governance. It says that the pastor consults the council and presides over the membership, which may include officials of the parish as well as other parishioners. Diocesan bishops may call for the establishment of such councils after consulting with their priests, and bishops prescribe the norms for them in their dioceses. Six out of thirteen guidelines for parish pastoral councils cite canon 536 as an official source in Vatican documents.[2]

At first glance canon 536 appears to mark a straightforward development from Vatican II, through the Circular Letter, up to the new Code. The pastoral council called for in canon 536 invites the laity's participation in the apostolate of the pastor.

OBSCURITIES OF THE CANON

Canon 536 obscures, however, the relation between the parish pastoral council and the Vatican II documents that had recommended councils. Consider, for example, canon 536 and the Decree on Bishops. By calling parish councils "pastoral," canon 536 signified that these councils were of the same kind as the councils recommended in the Bishops Decree. But canon 536 did not apply to parish pastoral councils the threefold description of their task from paragraph 27 of the decree.[3] Canon 536 did not say that the parish pastoral council is to study and reflect about pastoral matters and to recommend to the pastor its conclusions. This omission has had unfortunate consequences for Catholic efforts to understand councils. Recall that none of the thirteen guidelines for parish pastoral councils surveyed in chapter 1 explicitly cite paragraph 27 of the Bishops Decree.[4] Few realize the debt that parish pastoral councils owe to that decree.

Instead canon 536 described the council's task using an ambiguous formula, i.e., "to assist in fostering pastoral activity." This formula could refer to a type of activity or to the activity of the pastor.[5] Pastoral activity could be defined as "not having to do with administration." Or it could refer to what pastors do. Because of this ambiguity, the formula obscured the distinctive responsibility of the pastoral council. It left many with the mistaken impression that the council's task is no more specific than that of any other parish group that helps the pastor. Catholics with a stake in pastoral councils need to grasp the correct understanding of that phrase, as we shall see below.

Canon 536 had nothing to say about the Vatican II document most often cited as the source of parish councils, namely, paragraph 26 of the Decree on the Laity.[6] This paragraph had recommended councils "to assist the Church's apostolic work." It had said that such councils "can take care of the mutual coordinating of the various lay associations and undertakings." It was the sole reference to councils at the parish level in the documents of Vatican II.

When canon 536 legislated about parish pastoral councils, however, it did not even allude to the Laity Decree. This puzzled council members who studied canon 536 in terms of what they knew from Vatican II. Canon 536 said nothing about the apostolate of the laity. It said nothing about parish councils coordinating lay organizations. The canon left people wondering what (if any) relationship existed between Vatican II and the Code of Canon Law.[7]

EXPLAINING CANON 536

Several commentators in the 1980s and early 1990s tried without complete success to explain the new legislation recommending parish pastoral councils. Some argued that Vatican II had intended parish councils of the "pastoral" type from the start. Such councils were implicit (they said) in the reference to diocesan pastoral councils contained in the Decree on Bishops (par. 27). This point of view is not far from the truth, given the fact that the Bishops Decree, as the origin for pastoral councils in general, must also be the origin of parish pastoral councils. But Vatican II never said anything about pastoral councils at the parish level.

Some commentators argued that the intentions of the Vatican II bishops were misinterpreted.[8] It was a popular view but mistaken, they said, to quote paragraph 26 of the Decree on the Laity as the source of parish councils.[9] The argument of these commentators makes apparent sense, in light of subsequent documents. They have canonized pastoral councils, but few have ever mentioned apostolic councils. Yet it remains unarguably true that Laity Decree 26 is the only Vatican II decree that mentioned councils at the parochial level.

What is the correct view about the Laity Decree and its call for councils? Commentators disagree. They variously say that Laity Decree 26 called for councils on individual apostolic activities, or for councils to coordinate diocesan institutions, or for councils to coordinate autonomous apostolates.[10] These points of view conflict with one another. The commentators agree, however, that paragraph 26 did not refer to councils for the coordination of the parish. The pioneers who believed that it did refer to such coordination were mistaken.

The Vatican II bishops did not want *parish* councils (that is, councils for the lay apostolate). No, said these commentators, the bishops wanted *pastoral* councils (councils to assist the apostolate of pastors). The true intention of Vatican II, said the commentators, became clearer only gradually. The commentators hypothesized a period of experimentation following the Second Vatican Council.[11] This period of experimentation bore fruit in the 1973 Circular Letter. The letter affirmed that pastoral councils, which Vatican II had established for dioceses, were the kind of councils intended for the parish. The process of evolution culminated in the 1983 Code of Canon Law, which in canon 536 brought the development to legislation. According to some commentators, canon 536 put into law what the bishops of Vatican II had wanted all along.[12]

SELECTIVITY AND INNOVATION

The truth of the matter, however, is that canon 536 never clearly defined the relation between parish pastoral councils and the teaching of Vatican II. Rather, the canon was selective and innovative in its treatment of the Vatican II documents. It was selective in that it referred to the "pastoral" councils from the Bishops Decree, but not to the "apostolate" councils from the Laity Decree. Experience had shown that the language of Laity Decree 26 about councils "coordinating" lay initiatives was ambiguous. Canon 536 made it clear that pastoral councils do not coordinate parish initiatives—if by "coordinate" we mean that councils are legislative or executive bodies with an authority independent of the pastor. Avoiding references to Laity Decree 26, canon 536 left the "apostolate" or lay coordinating councils in limbo. And in fact, references to them in subsequent Vatican documents virtually disappeared.[13]

Canon 536 was innovative as well as selective. It innovated by calling for pastoral councils at the parish level, something never mentioned in the documents of Vatican II.[14] With this innovation, canon 536 linked parish councils to the apostolate of the pastor. He presides. He consults. He asks the council's help in fostering pastoral activity. This does not refer to activity that is more explicitly prayerful, or that discerns in order to reach consensus, or whose subject matter is spiritual rather than temporal. These popular misconceptions, as we saw in chapter ten, miss the point.

When canon 536 refers to the council giving its help in fostering pastoral activity, it alludes to the pastor's apostolate or mission. *Correctly understood, the term* pastoral activity *means whatever is connected to the office of the pastor.* To be sure, he can and should be attentive to the voice of the laity. His apostolate is the leadership of the parish community. Pastoral councils, however, do not exist primarily to guarantee the laity's right to be heard. Their focus is not the lay apostolate. No, councillors serve the apostolate of the pastor, helping him to make wise decisions. Canon 536 gives him enormous freedom to consult precisely to achieve this goal of wisdom. The pastor is not obliged to take the advice of the council.[15] Canon 536 states that the council possesses a consultative vote only. But the pastor consults for no other reason than to benefit from the council's study, reflection, and conclusions.

Commentators were mistaken to say that the first generation after Vatican II, the generation that established parish councils, had generally misinterpreted the conciliar documents. That generation was trying to implement a new ecclesial structure for which it had little guidance. Canon 536 did not simply make plain what was already present in the documents of Vatican II. It made selective and innovative use of those documents. By legislating for parish pastoral councils, it canonized the pastoral council idea and neglected the concept of lay apostolate councils. In retrospect, and in light of subsequent Vatican documents, we can say that the Vatican II source for parish pastoral councils is the idea first advanced in paragraph 27 of the Decree on Bishops. Guidelines for councils published by dioceses should refer primarily to the Bishops Decree as the source for pastoral councils, and only secondarily to canon 536.

CANON 536 AND VATICAN II

Prior to 1983, when the new Code of Canon Law was published, almost no one spoke of parish "pastoral" councils. The possibility of such councils, merely acknowledged in 1973's Circular Letter from the Congregation for the Clergy, was virtually unknown to council practitioners. But with the 1983 Code, the Catholic world had to interpret new legislation. Canon 536 called for parish "pastoral" councils, but did not use the language of Vatican II's Decree on Bishops. Instead of seeing there the threefold definition from Vatican II, readers of canon 536 could only conclude that the pastoral council was "to assist in fostering pastoral activity." This phrase was vague. Its relation to Bishops Decree 27 was unclear. It made no reference to Laity Decree 26. And one could not tell whether "pastoral" was a type of activity or a reference to the pastor.

For this reason it is unwise to refer exclusively to canon 536 as the source of the parish pastoral council. Because canon 536 was selective and innovative in the way it applied the teaching of Vatican II, one should always supplement references to canon 536 with an acknowledgment of paragraph 27 from the Decree on Bishops. There (with the amplification of the 1973 Circular Letter by the Congregation for the Clergy) we find the true source of the parish pastoral council.

Now we know that the "pastoral" council is a type of council first recommended in the Decree on Bishops regarding the pastor's apostolate. That apostolate is parish leadership. The council supports this apostolate through its work of study, reflection, and recommendation. Subsequent Vatican documents have endorsed this point of view, and to those documents we now turn.

NOTES

1. *Code of Canon Law*, reprinted in Beal et al., eds., *New Commentary on the Code of Canon Law*, 708. The commentary on cc. 515–552 is by John A. Renken.

2. See the guidelines for Scranton (10, 17), Charlotte (507, n. 16), Nashville (13), Youngstown (3), Rockford (2), and Gaylord (13, 15, 25). The 1996 guidelines from Great Falls–Billings also refer to c. 536 (1).

3. However, c. 511, about diocesan pastoral councils, did utilize the threefold description of the council's task.

4. See chap. 8, n. 13.

5. The Latin is *ad actionem pastoralem fovendam suum adiutorium praestent*, that is, to lend its help in encouraging, cherishing, or supporting (literally, "warming") pastoral activity.

6. For references to Laity Decree 26, see chap. 9, n. 9.

7. For a more complete analysis of the relation between c. 536 and the Vatican II documents, see Fischer, "What Was Vatican II's Intent?"

8. The late Bishop John R. Keating of the Diocese of Arlington argued that people misinterpreted the bishops of Vatican II when they assumed that the Decree on the Laity, par. 26 [which called for "apostolate" council at many levels, including the parish] was a call for parish councils. He wrote, "Commentators on Vatican II are agreed that this reference really does not speak of parish councils." See Keating, "Consultation in the Parish," 260 quoted here. But as we have seen (chap. 9, nn. 10–11), an entire host of writers did cite Laity Decree 26 as the source of parish councils.

9. Kim (73) said that the Vatican II basis for parish councils was merely a "popular assumption." Orville Griese said that this assumption was popular but mistaken ("The New Code of Canon Law and Parish Councils," *Homiletic and Pastoral Review* 85:4 [January 1985]: 47–53, 47 quoted here). He apologized (in n. 1) for making the same mistake himself in an earlier article (see O. Griese, "Pastor–Parish Council Collaboration," *The Priest* 33:2 [February 1977]: 19–22, 24).

10. These are the theories respectively of Griese ("The New Code," 48), of Keating (259), and of Kim (92) and Renken ("Pastoral Councils," 148).

11. Griese stated ("The New Code," 48) that "in a certain evolutionary process, however, and apparently in imitation of the diocesan pastoral council, parish pastoral councils came into being." Renken wrote ("Pastoral Councils," 138) that the "circular letter expanded earlier documents and related, at least to some degree, the Church's experience of pastoral councils." Kim said that parish pastoral councils were not a departure from Vatican II (138). Rather, they were "a consequence of experiments validating their [the pastoral councils'] existence" (38).

12. Griese stated ("The New Code," 52) that "the prescriptions of the new Code of Canon Law...follow closely the concepts...from the documents of Vatican II."

13. Paragraph 26 of the Laity Decree was not wholly ignored in the period between Vatican II and the new Code. John Renken has noted that, in the preparation of the 1983 Code of Canon Law, paragraph 26 was linked to parish pastoral councils (see Renken, "Pastoral Councils," 141, footnote 3). The *coetus* or discussion of parish pastoral councils by the pontifical commission for the interpretation of canon law on April 19, 1980, referred to paragraph 26 as a source (see *Communicationes* 13 (1981), 146). But after

the publication of the Code, there have been few references to Laity 26 in official Vatican documents. For a discussion of scholarly references to Laity 26 in light of canon 536, see chap. 9, footnote 11.

14. Pastoral councils at the parish level were first recommended in *Omnes Christifideles*, the 1973 Circular Letter from the Congregation to the Clergy, which was discussed in chap. 10.

15. Some may object to the proviso that the councils have a "consultative-only" vote (see, for example, chap. 7 above, nn. 3 and 4). But the consultative nature of the pastoral council does not leave the members without recourse when a pastor consults in bad faith or otherwise mistreats his people. Richard C. Cunningham describes the moral power of the laity in this way: "Ultimately they still possess the power of numbers, of finances, of public opinion, of *sensus fidelium*, of conscience and the radical power of shaking the dust from their feet as they exit." Richard C. Cunningham, "The Laity in the Revised Code," in James H. Provost, ed., *Code, Community, Ministry: Selected Studies for the Parish Minister Introducing the Revised Code of Canon Law* (Washington, DC: Canon Law Society of America, 1992), 32–37, at 37.

CHAPTER 12

The Uneven Documents
from 1987 to 2001

The previous four chapters have sketched the parish pastoral council in light of the official teaching of the Church:

Chapter 8 described the parish pastoral council as a parochial type of council first recommended for dioceses, the council that investigates and ponders the pastoral situation under the pastor's direction and recommends its findings to him.

Chapter 9 identified the Vatican II Decree on Bishops—and not the Decree on the Apostolate of Lay People—as the proper source for parish pastoral councils.

Chapter 10 defined the term *pastoral* as pertaining to the apostolate of pastors, and not to the council's prayerfulness, style of meeting, or decision-making procedure.

Chapter 11 interpreted the phrase from canon 536 about how councillors "assist in fostering pastoral activity" as meaning that they help the pastor make wise practical decisions in light of the pastoral council's threefold task.

These chapters construe the council's role in a very precise way. The main work of pastoral councils is not the broad coordination of parish committees, not a vague and unfocused assistance to the pastor, not the articulation of exclusively lay concerns. No, its main work is pastoral planning. The council plans when the pastor invites the members to study some aspect of the parish situation, to reflect on it, and to recommend their findings. This was the path sketched out for diocesan pastoral councils in 1965, extended to parish pastoral councils in 1973, and legislated in 1983.

Chapter 8's survey of thirteen pastoral council guidelines from dioceses throughout the United States, however, does not corroborate this precise interpretation of the council role. We saw that council guidelines rarely give a concise answer to the question of what councils are to do. Undoubtedly, most guidelines affirm that pastoral planning is the duty of councils. But many burden the council with additional duties, such as the implementation of policies and the coordination of standing committees, duties that stand outside the council's main responsibilities. These compete with and may obscure the council's primary role as pastoral planner—the role assigned to councils by official Vatican documents in the 1960s, 1970s, and 1980s.

The dissonance between these early Vatican documents and the more recent council guidelines published by U.S. dioceses presents a problem. Does the definition of *pastoral councils* in the Vatican II and immediate postconciliar documents still hold? Is the main role of pastoral councils the threefold role of investigating, pondering, and reaching conclusions? Or has that precise role been expanded in later documents from the 1980s, 1990s, and the new millennium? What have the newer documents added to the Church's official teaching about pastoral councils?

To answer these questions, we shall look at six Vatican documents that have emerged since the 1983 publication of the Code of Canon Law. The two most recent documents soundly affirm our general thesis about Vatican II's Decree on Bishops as the first and best source for understanding the parish *pastoral council*. They are the 2002 Instruction by the Sacred Congregation for the Clergy, entitled "The Priest, Pastor and Leader of the Parish Community," and the 2004 Directory for the Pastoral Ministry of Bishops, entitled *Apostolorum successores*. They will be the topics of chapter 13.

Four older documents, whose testimony to the Vatican II origin of the parish pastoral council is somewhat uneven, also deserve our attention:

> *Christifideles laici* (1987), Pope John Paul II's Apostolic
> Exhortation on the Laity;
> *Ecclesiae de mysterio* (1997), an Instruction signed by six
> Vatican Congregations and two Pontifical Councils;

Ecclesia in Asia (1999), an Apostolic Exhortation by Pope
   John Paul II based on the Assembly for Asia of the Synod
   of Bishops;
Novo millennio ineunte (2001), an Apostolic Letter of Pope
   John Paul II on the new millennium.

Each one of these documents considers the pastoral council at
some length, but in different ways and with differing degrees of thor-
oughness. Although they do not deny the foundation of the parish pastoral council in Vatican II's Decree on Bishops (par. 27), they are
uneven in their testimony to it. They remain important witnesses, however, to the evolution of our understanding of the pastoral council.

CHRISTIFIDELES LAICI

Let us begin with a consideration of *Christifideles laici*,[1] Pope
John Paul II's Apostolic Exhortation based on the 1987 World Synod
of Bishops. *Christifideles* has a brief reference to diocesan pastoral
councils in paragraph 25 and to parish pastoral councils in paragraph
27. These references speak positively about pastoral councils, but do
not describe them in the language of their proper source, i.e., the
Vatican II Decree on Bishops.

Paragraph 25 of *Christifideles* enthusiastically says that the
diocesan pastoral council (DPC) "could be the principal form of collaboration, dialogue and discernment." Other forms can accomplish
these purposes (the document implies), but among them, the DPC
may be foremost. The sentence appears to give the DPC three significant responsibilities—collaboration, dialogue, and discernment—but it does not assign these responsibilities to the pastoral
council in an exclusive or unambiguous way. From this passage, we
do not know precisely how laypeople are to participate in pastoral
councils.

Paragraph 25 bravely adds that the "participation" of laypeople
in the DPC "can broaden resources in consultation and the principle
of collaboration and in certain instances also in decision making." Lay
participation certainly broadens a bishop's resources. Now, with a pastoral council (the document implies), he has an official consultative

body that includes laypeople, broader than the diocesan curia. They can collaborate with the bishop and help him in making decisions.

Unfortunately, "participation" hardly describes the pastoral council's main role. The threefold role as described in the 1965 Decree on Bishops (which states that the pastoral council investigates, ponders, and recommends conclusions) is more precise. A bishop has many resources for collaboration and consultation, of which the DPC is but one. By describing the pastoral council in terms of functions that other bodies in the church may perform, and by ignoring the council's threefold responsibility as defined at Vatican II, *Christifideles* shines but a dim light on the DPC. It appears to enhance the council's role (saying that it "could be the principal form") without saying much that is definite.

Paragraph 27 of *Christifideles* is about parish pastoral councils. The guidelines for the Dioceses of Youngstown and of Sacramento cite it.[2] The paragraph states that the purpose of the parish pastoral council is "examining and solving pastoral problems 'by general discussion.'" This last phrase is a quotation from the Decree on the Laity (par. 10). It suggests that the study and solution of problems, described in the 1965 decree, is the task of the parish pastoral council, which was not explicitly recommended until 1973. To that extent, the suggestion is an anachronism. Still, the method of "general discussion" well describes the second task of the pastoral council, the task of pondering or reflection on what the council has investigated.

The reference in *Christifideles* to the Laity Decree may mislead the reader to conclude that parish pastoral councils serve the apostolate of the laity, that is, the apostolate of service to the world. But this is not the case. Pastoral councils serve the apostolate of pastors, as described in the Decree on Bishops. This is the apostolate of church leadership. So the use of *Christifideles* in the Youngstown and Sacramento guidelines does not reinforce our contention that the Decree on Bishops (with its emphasis on the pastor's apostolate) is the proper Vatican II source for councils. The Bishops Decree defines the work of the pastoral council as "investigation, pondering, and recommendation." This is more precise than the reference from the Laity Decree to "general discussion." *Christifideles* misleadingly points the reader to the lay apostolate, when it should have pointed to the pastoral apostolate.

ECCLESIAE DE MYSTERIO
AND ECCLESIA IN ASIA

Two Vatican documents since 1973 refer to parish pastoral councils, but are not cited in any of the thirteen diocesan guidelines that we examined in chapter 8. *Ecclesiae de mysterio* was an Instruction from 1997 signed by six Vatican congregations.[3] Cautious in tone, this 1997 Instruction answers "Certain Questions Regarding Collaboration of the Non-Ordained Faithful in the Sacred Ministry of Priest." The document basically teaches what pastoral councils are *not*. It states that:

They enjoy a consultative vote only and cannot in any way become deliberative structures (§2).
If the pastor does not preside over the council, its deliberations are "null and void" (§3).
Pastoral councils that have arisen in the past must be made to conform to the Church's law in the present (§5).

In short, the document warns that people who believe that pastoral councils might take the place of pastors are mistaken. Councillors collaborate in the pastor's ministry, but do not replace it.

The negative tone of *Ecclesiae de mysterio* clearly implies a warning. It warns people that pastoral councils in the past may have been falsely construed. Some may have wrongly concluded that pastoral councils are deliberative structures that can legislate for the parish. Some may have assumed that such councils exist independently of their pastor. Some may have believed that pastoral councils are not governed by the Church's law. *Ecclesiae de mysterio* wants to set the record straight. Although its tone is cautious, the document affirms the basic view of pastoral councils first proposed in the Bishops Decree and later affirmed in official Vatican publications. The document implies that pastors consult the council but are not bound by its recommendations.

Ecclesia in Asia,[4] Pope John Paul II's 1999 Apostolic Exhortation to the bishops of Asia, is a third document that sheds light on the topic of pastoral councils. The new light emerges from its description of a somewhat decentralized Asian Church. The Exhortation describes the diocese as a "community of communities," that is, a union of parishes, each of which accomplishes its own pastoral planning through councils. The key sentence occurs in paragraph 25:

> There is a need to foster greater involvement of the laity and consecrated men and women in pastoral planning and decision making through such participatory structures as pastoral councils and parish assemblies.

The use of the phrase "pastoral planning" is remarkable as a synonym for the work of councils. Although there is a precedent for the use of the phrase,[5] nevertheless it is relatively uncommon in official documents. *Ecclesia in Asia* does not define pastoral planning, but such planning can be seen as an abbreviation for the threefold task of study, reflection, and recommendation, the threefold task from the Decree on Bishops.

The 1999 Exhortation refers to the pastoral council and the parish assembly as "participatory structures." This phrase is vague as a description of councils (as we saw in connection with *Christifideles laici*). It does not say how people are to participate. Perhaps it is meant as a counter-concept to the phrase "deliberative structures," which *Ecclesiae de mysterio* flatly said that pastoral councils are not. If *participative* means "not deliberative," the word simply affirms that pastoral councils allow for broad participation, but possess a consultative-only vote.

But the 1999 Exhortation says more than that. It also speaks of a "participatory church" in which "every member's unique charism needs to be acknowledged, developed, and effectively utilized" (par. 25). In brief, *Ecclesia in Asia* suggests that no Christian should passively sit on the sidelines. Everyone has a contribution to make. Councils allow for the participation of the faithful, states the Exhortation, in the apostolate of the pastor. How they participate, however, remains unclear. *Ecclesia in Asia* does not use the threefold description from the Bishops Decree about the pastoral council's role. The use of this description could have made more precise the Exhortation's insistence upon the involvement of people in "pastoral planning." In *Ecclesia in Asia*, however, the term remains undefined.

NOVO MILLENNIO

Finally let us consider *Novo millennio ineunte*, Pope John Paul II's 2001 Apostolic Letter "at the beginning of the new millennium." The Scranton diocesan guidelines for pastoral councils refer to *Novo millennio* at a number of places.[6] They do so in order to make three points. First, pastoral councils may aid in evangelization; second, councils need not seek a "new program" but should instead translate the gospel into pastoral initiatives; and third, the goal of councils is the achievement of a "spirituality of communion."[7] Although *Novo millennio* does not relate these three points to pastoral councils explicitly, the Scranton guidelines do. We can conclude that each of these three points indicates possibilities inherent in the pastoral council. Unfortunately, however, *Novo millennio* does not link the origin of pastoral councils to the Vatican II Decree on Bishops. Because it does not use the decree's more precise language, the 2001 Apostolic Letter sheds little light on the fundamental purpose of pastoral councils.

Surprisingly, the Scranton diocesan guidelines ignore paragraph 45 of *Novo millennio*, the only paragraph which treats pastoral councils in an explicit way. Paragraph 45 describes councils as "structures of participation." We have already encountered the word *participation* in relation to pastoral councils in *Christifideles laici* and *Ecclesia in Asia*. There we said that this word is ambiguous, because it does not describe how laypeople are to participate in councils. To be sure, paragraph 45 of *Novo millennio* says that canon law offers "precise rules for participation" in pastoral councils. It never defines those rules, however, so the paragraph is confusing.[8] Pastoral councils may be structures for participation, but the paragraph does not say who participates or how.

Despite that shortcoming, paragraph 45 of *Novo millennio* does endorse the pastoral council as a place of "fruitful dialogue." Pastoral councils, as structures of participation, are a means for cultivating and extending communion. The paragraph even quotes St. Benedict and St. Paulinus of Nola, suggesting that these two saints consulted "with the entire People of God" and can be a model for pastors today. That being said, *Novo millennio* sheds no more light on the origin and specific purpose of pastoral councils than does *Christifideles laici* or

Ecclesia in Asia. To be sure, the term *participation* may well describe the layperson's role in the pastor's apostolate. But the term is too vague to explain how the council participates.

THE PRECISE DEFINITION HOLDS

At the start of this chapter, we saw that an analysis of Vatican documents from 1965–83 yields a rather precise description of the task of the pastoral council. It is the task of investigating and pondering matters under the pastor's direction and recommending to him the council's conclusions. The main focus of councils is not the apostolate of the laity with its mission to the world, but the apostolate of the pastor. The council helps him to make wise decisions on behalf of the church he represents.

Chapters 8–11 have shown, however, that diocesan guidelines for pastoral councils do not unanimously embrace this precise description of the council role. The guidelines rarely cite the *Decree on Bishops* as the foundation of pastoral councils and frequently misunderstand councils as an expression of the lay apostolate. Comparing what diocesan guidelines say about councils to the Vatican portrait of councils, one can hardly avoid the conclusion that the pastoral council is widely misunderstood, and that the typical council is hardly pastoral.

This chapter has asked how the four Vatican documents from 1987–2001 *have* added to our understanding of the pastoral council. The answer depends on the document that one reads.

> *Christifideles laici* adopts an appreciative tone, saying what the pastoral council "could be," but adds nothing new to our fundamental understanding.
>
> *Ecclesiae in mysterio* cautions against misunderstanding the pastoral council, reminding readers of what it is not.
>
> *Ecclesia in Asia* reflects a vision of the Church as a community of communities for which the pastoral council is an instrument of participation and planning.
>
> *Novo millennio ineunte* describes councils as structures of participation, but remains vague about how people participate or in what they are participating.

These four documents do not uniformly reinforce our contention that the Vatican II Decree on Bishops is the charter of the pastoral council. One document (*Christifideles*) even cites the Decree on Laity as a source for parish pastoral councils, anachronistically applying the language of 1965 to a structure that was not explicitly recommended until 1973. Three documents speak of the pastoral council as a structure of participation and neglect its fundamental nature. In short, the four recent documents are uneven in value.

With that concession in mind, however, we can still affirm the precise definition of the pastoral council from Vatican II. None of the four documents from 1987–2001 explicitly rejects the source of pastoral councils in the Decree on Bishops. Vatican II assigned to pastoral councils the role of investigating, pondering, and reaching conclusions—a role that deserves to be called pastoral planning. That is what makes the pastoral council truly pastoral. This view of the pastoral council is amply and explicitly affirmed in the two most recent Vatican documents to treat the pastoral council, to which we now turn.

NOTES

1. Pope John Paul II, *Christifideles laici* (Apostolic Exhortation on the Laity), based on the 1987 World Synod of Bishops, January 30, 1987, *Origins* 18:35 (Feb. 9, 1989): 561, 653–595.

2. The Youngstown guidelines quote *Christifideles* on p. 3, and the Sacramento guidelines quote it on p. 1. The phrase "by general discussion" is a quote from Vatican II's *Apostolicam actuositatem*, no. 10.

3. *Ecclesiae de mysterio* (Instruction on Certain Questions Regarding Collaboration of the Non-Ordained Faithful in the Sacred Ministry of Priest), written by a committee consisting of representatives of the Congregation for the Clergy, the Pontifical Council for the Laity, the Congregation for the Doctrine of the Faith, the Congregation for Divine Worship and the Discipline of the Sacraments, the Congregation for Bishops, the Congregation for the Evangelization of Peoples, the Congregation for Institutes of Consecrated Life and Societies of Apostolic Life, and the Pontifical Council for the Interpretation of Legislative Texts. Approved *in forma specifica* by Pope John Paul II and promulgated on August 15, 1997. Downloaded from the official Vatican Web site, http://www.vatican.va/roman_curia/pontifical_councils/laity/documents/rc_con_interdic_doc_15081997_en.html (accessed on October 12, 2007).

4. *Ecclesia in Asia*, Apostolic Exhortation of Pope John Paul II presented in New Delhi, India, on November 6, 1999, to more than 100 Asian Bishops. It is based on the work of the April 19–May 14, 1998, Special Assembly for Asia of the Synod of Bishops, one of the regional synods called for by the pope as part of preparations for the Jubilee Year 2000. Downloaded from http://www.vatican.va/holy_father/john_paul_ii/apost_exhortations/documents/hf_jp-ii_exh_06111999_ecclesia-in-asia_en.html (accessed November 2, 2007).

5. There is a reference to "pastoral planning" in a document from the Sacred Congregation for Bishops, *Ecclesiae imago* (Directory on the Pastoral Ministry of Bishops, May 31, 1973) translation prepared by the Benedictine monks of the Seminary of Christ the King, Mission, British Columbia (Ottawa: Publications Service of the Canadian Catholic Conference, 1974). In par. 204 we read, "The pastoral council...furnishes the judgments necessary to enable the diocesan community to plan its pastoral program systematically and to fulfill it effectively."

6. Scranton guidelines, 4, 6–7, and 12. For *Novo millennio's* reference to evangelization, see the Scranton guidelines, 4. For *Novo millennio's* recommendation (at par. 29) about translating the gospel (rather than creating a "new program"), see the Scranton guidelines, 7. Here the Scranton guidelines do not cite *Novo millennio* directly, but instead cite *Ecclesia de Eucharistia* (Pope John Paul II's 2003 Encyclical Letter on the Eucharist), which quotes *Novo millennio*. For *Novo millennio's* reference (at par. 43) to the "spirituality of communion," see the Scranton guidelines, 12.

7. Pope John Paul II, *Novo millennio ineunte* (At the Beginning of the New Millennium), Apostolic Letter of January 6, 2001. Available at http://www.vatican.va/holy_father/john_paul_ii/apost_letters/documents/hf_jp-ii_apl_20010106_novo-millennio-ineunte_en.html (accessed on September 11, 2007).

8. Paragraph 45 of *Novo millennio* states that the council of priests and the pastoral council "are not governed by rules of parliamentary democracy, because they are consultative rather than deliberative" (with a footnote reference to *Ecclesia de mysterio*, §5). *Ecclesia de mysterio* is the document whose cautious warnings we have already discussed. Perhaps the passage from *Ecclesia de mysterio*, which emphasized that pastoral and finance councils are governed by canon law, is meant to reinforce the "precise rules for participation." This does not repudiate parliamentary procedure, but reminds the reader that councils do not legislate.

CHAPTER 13

The Documents of 2002 and 2004

In 2002 and 2004 the Vatican Congregations for the Clergy and for Bishops issued two documents that treated the pastoral council in considerable detail. These two documents both affirmed the 1965 Decree on Bishops (and not the Decree on Lay People) as the foundation of the pastoral council. In other words, they viewed the pastoral council as the type of council that, under the pastor's direction, investigates, considers, and recommends its conclusions. These two new documents are thus more precise than the documents from 1987 to 2001 that we examined in the last chapter.

The documents from 1987 to 2001 somewhat vaguely had defined the pastoral council in terms of "planning" and "participation." The documents from 2002 and 2004 also use those words, but relate them to the pastoral council's Vatican II origins. In other words, pastoral councillors plan and participate by performing the threefold task of investigating, considering, and recommending conclusions. The newer documents also support our thesis that the pastoral council mainly serves, not the lay apostolate, but the apostolate of the pastor.

THE 2002 INSTRUCTION

Let us begin by looking at the Congregation for the Clergy's 2002 Instruction entitled "The Priest, Pastor and Leader of the Parish Community." This document explicitly links the parish pastoral council and the diocesan pastoral council. They are both instances of the one type, the "pastoral" council recommended in Vatican II's Decree on Bishops. It is the council with the threefold planning role of investigation, reflection, and recommending conclusions. The 2002 Instruction puts it this way:

> The basic task of such a [parish pastoral] council is to serve, at institutional level, the orderly collaboration of the faithful in the development of pastoral activity which is proper to priests. The pastoral council is thus a *consultative* organ in which the faithful, expressing their baptismal responsibility, can assist the parish priest, who presides at the council, by offering their advice on pastoral matters.[1]

The phrase "proper to priests" clarifies the meaning of the word *pastoral*. The word does not signify a prayerful focus, a discerning style, or a spiritual content, but rather a specific apostolate. The pastoral council exists to aid the apostolate of the pastor by developing the "pastoral" activity proper to him.

What is this activity? The 2002 Instruction from the Congregation for the Clergy quotes the seven examples in the congregation's 1973 Circular Letter to bishops, the letter we examined in chapter 10. The seven examples of pastoral activity are:

> To provide proposals and suggestions on (1) missionary, (2) catechetical, and (3) apostolic initiatives;
> To advise pastors concerning the promotion of (4) doctrinal formation and (5) the sacramental life of the faithful;
> To make recommendations (6) concerning pastoral activities to help the parish in the various social and territorial areas;
> To offer suggestions (7) concerning public opinion on matters pertaining to the Church.[2]

These illustrations reinforce the threefold pastoral planning role of the pastoral council. The council exists to make wise recommendations after study and reflection. The seven illustrations also suggest that the council's job is consultative. The council does not supervise or coordinate committees, but puts its efforts at the service of the pastor who consults it. The word *coordination*, drawn from the 1965 Decree on Lay People, has often been misapplied to pastoral councils. They are occasionally regarded as the coordinators of parish committees.[3] Lay apostolate councils were indeed envisioned as the coordinators of lay initiatives. But coordination is not pastoral planning, the task of pastoral council. Planning means the spiritual and intellectual task of seeking wisdom, not the executive or managerial task of directing lay groups.

The 2002 Instruction emphasizes this last point. Describing the relation between the parish priest and his parishioners as one of "mutual service," the Instruction says that the pastor consults the council and presides at its meetings:

> It would therefore be senseless to consider the pastoral council as an organ replacing the parish priest in his government of the parish, or as one which, on the basis of a majority vote, materially constrains the parish priest in his direction of the parish.[4]

In other words, the parish priest is the legal representative of the parish. To say that the parish pastoral council is a "leadership body" or a "leadership structure" (as some modern authors do[5]) can be misleading. The council cannot "materially constrain" (that is, overrule) the pastor. Furthermore, he has the freedom to consult as he sees fit. No one can tell him what practical matters he can or cannot consult about.[6] If he chooses to consult about catechetical, administrative, apostolic, financial, or public relations matters, he can do so.

In short, the 2002 Instruction from the Congregation for the Clergy lends support to our precise definition of the parish pastoral council. The pastor consults the council to help him plan for the parish. He does so by asking the council to assume the threefold role first defined in the 1965 Decree on Bishops. In 1973, the Congregation for the Clergy extended Vatican II's recommendations about diocesan pastoral councils to parish pastoral councils. The Congregation's 2002 Instruction reaffirms that view. Pastoral councillors fulfill their task by offering the pastor wise recommendations based on investigation and reflection.

The Instruction is a relatively recent document. Only a single diocesan guideline of the thirteen we surveyed in chapter 8 quotes from it.[7] For that reason, the 2002 Instruction has not yet had much effect on pastoral council guidelines in the United States. Is its view of the pastoral council representative of the thinking of the wider Church?

One might speculate that the understanding expressed in the 2002 Instruction is no more representative of the Church's thinking than any of the four uneven documents from 1987 to 2001 that were reviewed in chapter 12. But two facts weigh against that view. The first is that the Instruction recapitulates an interpretation of the pastoral council that was first expressed in 1965 and reaffirmed in five documents from that point until 1983.[8] The second fact is that the 2002 interpretation was underscored in a 2004 Directory for the Pastoral Ministry of Bishops, which will be discussed next. In light of these two facts, the views expressed in 2002 and 2004 assume greater weight.

THE 2004 DIRECTORY

In 2004 the Vatican's Congregation for Bishops issued a Directory for the Pastoral Ministry of Bishops (*Apostolorum successores*).[9] Its interpretation of the pastoral council follows the main line that extends from Vatican II up to the 2002 Instruction. The Directory mentions pastoral councils in three paragraphs,[10] one of which is devoted entirely to them. Paragraph 184 sketches the council's purpose, membership, meetings, scope, and preparation. Let us consider each of these in turn.

Purpose

Although paragraph 184 says that the pastoral council expresses the "participation" of the faithful, and although it mentions a diocesan "pastoral plan," nevertheless the purpose of the council is not described as participation or planning. No, the Directory defines the purpose of the council in the threefold terminology of Vatican II with a footnote reference to the Decree on Bishops, par. 27. Earlier documents had spoken of participation and planning[11] without explaining what they meant. The Directory puts these into the context of Vatican II.

Membership

The Directory gives the bishop a great deal of leeway in "electing" members. He can decide how to choose them and should lay out the method in a formal way, that is, by statutes. "He reserves to himself the right to exclude those who do not appear suitable," such as those who are not "in full communion with the Catholic Church,"

or those incapable of the threefold task of the council. Pastors consult councils, and they need to have to have confidence in those whom they are consulting.

Although the Directory states that the pastoral council does not "represent" the faithful in a juridical sense, nevertheless it is representative in two ways. First, the council "should *truly reflect* the entire portion of the People of God which constitutes the particular Church." Second, councillors should be chosen "with consideration given to the different areas of the diocese, social conditions and professions, and the role which they have in the apostolate whether individually or jointly."[12] What do these two passages say about representation? They suggest that the pastoral council need not reflect the exact demographic makeup of the diocese. Representation does not mean that the pastoral council membership exactly mirrors the ethnic, cultural, ideological, or geographical makeup of the church it serves. Despite that, the Directory implies, members should be chosen "with consideration" for demographic realities. They remain an important factor, one among others. In this way, the Directory avoids defining *representation* in terms of a political democracy or a demographic profile.[13]

Meetings

Paragraph 184 of the Directory gives to the bishop extraordinary power over the meetings of the council. It states that he "proposes the question to be treated, he chairs the meetings, he decides whether or not it is appropriate to publish the themes considered and he determines how to reach conclusions."[14] This passage goes beyond the stipulations of canon law.[15] Canon 514, §1 is silent about who proposes questions. It implicitly allows others besides the bishop to do so. It states only that the bishop presides. The canon does not address the question about whether others can chair the meeting. Finally, it says nothing about how the council is to reach conclusions. The canon states only that the council is to reach practical conclusions and propose them. The treatment of meetings in paragraph 184 of the Directory seems, at first glance, to be unduly restrictive.

The powers over the council granted to the bishop in the Directory do make explicit, however, what is implicit in the concept of a "pastoral" council. A bishop consults the pastoral council because he desires practical wisdom. He enlists the members' study and reflection in a project because he wants their prudent advice. He does not want to act until he is sure that a plan has been thoroughly considered. He is not consulting about how laypeople should exercise their apostolate in the world. No, he is considering his own apostolate, the apostolate of governance.[16] That suggests an explanation for the powers granted in the Directory to the bishop. He proposes the questions because they are his questions, the questions that he faces in his apostolate. He determines how to reach conclusions, because he is the one who will act on them.

Scope

The bishop has a great deal of latitude, according to paragraph 184, regarding what he may consult about. For example, he may discuss with the council themes relating to the "pastoral activity" of the diocese. This includes the "pastoral plan" (whose nature remains undefined in the Directory), diocesan initiatives, faith formation, and sacramental life, assistance for the clergy's pastoral ministry, and public relations.[17] In short, a bishop may consult about virtually any practical subject. Faith, orthodoxy, moral principles or laws of the universal Church are beyond the scope of the pastoral council,[18] but little else is off limits.

Preparation

By emphasizing the pastoral council's need to prepare for meetings, the Directory underscores the first of every council's three tasks, namely, the task of investigation. "For maximum effectiveness, the meetings of the council should be preceded by suitable preparation."[19] The pastoral council does not fulfill the purpose envisioned for it by the Church if it becomes merely a sounding board that engages in a conversation without prior study. Without investigating a topic prior to a dialogue, councillors have little on which to reflect or ponder. Preparation—the work of investigation, research, inquiry, reflection, analysis, and prayerful discernment—distinguishes the true pastoral council.

To sum up, the 2004 Directory affirms the "pastoral" nature of the pastoral council. It links the council to the apostolate of the bishop. The Directory emphasizes episcopal authority, submitting to the bishop the decision about how members are to be chosen, and allowing him to exclude members whom he believes to be unsuitable. The Directory reserves to the bishop the right to propose questions to the council. Moreover it states that "The pastoral council ceases when a diocese is vacant and it may be dissolved by the Bishop when it does not fulfill the tasks assigned to it."[20] The point is that the bishop consults the council. It does not exist as an administrative or managerial body independent of him. It serves his apostolate by its work of serious investigation, thorough reflection, and the recommendation of wise conclusions.

CONSEQUENCES FOR PASTORAL COUNCILS

The documents from 2002 and 2004 make explicit an understanding of the pastoral council that, in some respects, was merely latent prior to their publication. Before the 2002 Instruction and the 2004 Directory, one could have claimed that the Vatican II Decree on the Laity was a font or source for "parish" councils. One could even have argued that the addition of the word *pastoral* meant a parish council that refrained from questions of parish management or administration.[21] Scholars could cite a passage from the Vatican II documents in which the language of "coordination," usually linked to the lay apostolate council, was applied to the pastoral council.[22] They could also claim that the 1973 Directory on Bishops spoke of parish pastoral councils dedicated to the lay apostolate.[23] All of these citations provide some documentary evidence for the claim that the Decree on Bishops of Vatican II was not the only source for the pastoral council, and that the Decree on the Laity was a source as well.

That is why the two documents from 2002 and 2004 are so important. They lend their weight to an interpretation of the pastoral council that is well-founded and coherent. Indeed, they reprise an interpretation that goes back to Vatican II. According to this interpretation, the Decree on Bishops is the proper source of the pastoral council. It serves the apostolate of pastors (rather than the apostolate of laypeople). It undertakes pastoral planning and does not view itself as the coordinator of committees. The two documents clearly adopt this viewpoint.

For these reasons, the interpretation of the pastoral council by the 2002 Instruction and the 2004 Directory appears authoritative. The interpretation confirms a trajectory. The trajectory may wobble at times, given the ambiguity of the documents of Vatican II and the period leading up to the revised code. But the trajectory is generally true. It is plausible. It offers a persuasive and reasonably coherent view of the pastoral council. The features of this interpretation can be summarized as follows:

1. Purpose. The pastor invites the council's help in investigating, pondering, and reaching sound conclusions about some aspect of the pastoral situation.

2. Preparation. The council is more than a sounding board, and has the specific preparatory tasks of research and reflection.

3. Apostolate. The council aids the pastor's apostolate of leading the parish. It respects the autonomy of the lay apostolate of Christian service to the world.

4. The Pastor as Presider. The pastor is a presider, not a member. As the parish's legal representative, he wants to present the parish's wisdom to the world.

5. The Consultative Relationship. The pastor consults the council. He wants the benefit of the members' practical wisdom and prudence.

6. Membership. The pastor wants wise councillors—committed Christians with the capacity for study, for reflection, and for reaching sound conclusions.

7. Representation. The council is not a juridical representative of the church, but its makeup should reflect the church's locale, society, and apostolic endeavors.

8. Conclusion. The pastor determines how to reach conclusions in a particular sense: he decides when he no longer needs to consult about a particular issue.

These are the clear teachings of the 2002 Instruction and the 2004 Directory. Building upon the *Decree on Bishops*, and together with the documents reviewed in the past few chapters, they form a coherent interpretation of the pastoral council. The teachings are as relevant to the parish pastoral council as they are to its diocesan counterpart.

NOTES

1. Congregation for the Clergy, "The Priest, Pastor and Leader of the Parish Community," par. 26.

2. Ibid., quoting from the Congregation for the Clergy's *Omnes Christifideles* (Circular Letter on "Pastoral Councils"), par. 9.

3. See the discussion of the *Apostolicam actuositatem* (Decree on the Apostolate of Lay Persons), par. 26, in chap. 9 above, "Origins of the Pastoral Council."

4. Ibid.

5. Ferguson, 21; Gubish et al., 8.

6. See chap. 10 and its discussion of Congregation for the Clergy's Circular Letter *Omnes Christifideles*, par. 9.

7. The Scranton guidelines quote from "The Priest, Pastor and Leader" on 10.

8. These include *Ecclesiae Sanctae* I, the 1966 Apostolic Letter of Pope Paul VI on the Implementation of the Decree on Bishops, §16; *De Sacerdotio ministeriali*, the 1971 statement of the Synod of Bishops, at part 2, II, §3; *Ecclesiae imago*, the 1973 Directory on the Pastoral Ministry of Bishops, at par. 204; *Omnes Christifideles*, the 1973 Circular Letter of the Congregation for the Clergy, esp. at par. 9; and the Code of Canon Law, c. 511.

9. Congregation for Bishops, *Apostolorum successores* (Directory for the Pastoral Ministry of Bishops). The Directory describes itself as "an updated and revised edition" of the Congregation for Bishops' *Ecclesiae imago* (Directory on the Pastoral Ministry of Bishops), issued on February 22, 1973. A translation (dated May 31, 1973) was prepared by Benedictine monks of the Seminary of Christ the King, Mission, British Columbia (Ottawa: Publications Service of the Canadian Catholic Conference, 1974).

10. In par. 122, *Apostolorum successores* (Directory for the Pastoral Ministry of Bishops) states that a bishop may consult his pastoral council before issuing a general letter to his people. In par. 181, it states that the pastoral council may help the bishop study proposals put forward by his staff. Other study groups cannot replace or compete with the pastoral council (we read), because it is governed by the Church's law. There, in par. 181, the Directory links the diocesan pastoral council to the parish pastoral council. It states that "the pastoral council and the parish priest should fulfill their respective roles effectively, avoiding any hint of congregationalism" and cites cc. 519 (on the pastor's governance of the parish) and 536 (on the parish pastoral council). One can speculate that the warning against "congregationalism" is a warning against pastoral councils that wrongly presume that they are deliberative, rather than consultative. Finally, par. 184 is devoted entirely to the pastoral council.

11. On "participation," see the Congregation for the Clergy, *Christifideles laici* (Circular Letter on "Pastoral Councils") par. 25; John Paul II, *Ecclesia in Asia* (The Church in Asia) par. 25; and John Paul II, *Novo millennio ineunte* (At the Beginning) par. 45. On "planning," see *Ecclesia in Asia*, par. 25; and *Novo millennio ineunte*, par. 29. These are discussed in chap. 12 above, "Councils in Vatican Documents from 1987–2001."

12. Congregation for Bishops, *Apostolorum successores*, par. 184. The first passage paraphrases c. 212, §2, and the second passage is a direct quote. C. 212 borrows heavily from *Apostolorum successores*, the Congregation for the Clergy's 1973 Circular Letter, par. 7:

> As far as the composition of the pastoral council is concerned, although the members of the council cannot in a juridical sense be called representatives of the total diocesan community, nevertheless, as far as possible, they should present a witness or sign of the entire diocese, and, therefore, it seems extremely opportune that priests, religious and laity who expound various requirements and experiences take part in the council. The persons, then, appointed to the pastoral council ought to be selected in such a way that the entire composition of the People of God within the diocese is truly represented, taking into consideration the different regions, social conditions and professions as well as the parts which individuals and associations have in the apostolate, especially those who possess noteworthy prestige and prudence.

13. For a discussion of the selection of pastoral council members, see Mark F. Fischer and Sr. Rosalie Murphy, SNDdeN., "Selecting Effective Pastoral Council Members" (2004), posted in 2005 on the Web site of the United States Conference of Catholic Bishops, Secretariat for Family, Laity, Women and Youth: http://www.usccb.org/laity/pastoral.shtml.

14. To this passage is attached a footnote reference to c. 514, §1. The canon states that "It pertains exclusively to the diocesan bishop to convoke the pastoral council according to the necessities of the apostolate and to preside over it; the pastoral council enjoys only a consultative vote; it is for the bishop alone to make public what has been done in the council."

15. The passage in par. 184 goes beyond c. 514, §1 in several ways. First, the canon does not state that the bishop alone proposes the questions to be treated. Second, the canon does not address the question about who is to "chair" the pastoral council meetings. Because the Latin text of the Directory is not available online, one cannot say whether the verb *to chair* has been used to translate the Latin verb *to preside*. Third, the canon is silent about how the council is to reach conclusions.

16. The focus of the pastoral council on the bishop's own apostolate helps explain an allusion to the lay apostolate in par. 184 of the Directory (*Apostolorum successores*) of the Congregation for Bishops. Describing the pastoral council as "consultative," the Directory states that "It should always be characterized by proper respect both for Episcopal jurisdiction and for the autonomy of the faithful (as individuals or in associations). It should never claim the authority to direct or coordinate activities beyond its competence." This alludes to the 1965 Decree on the Apostolate of Lay People (*Apostolicam actuositatem*), which stated that lay apostolate councils "can take care of the mutual coordinating of the various lay associations and undertakings, the autonomy and particular nature of each remaining untouched" (par. 26). In other words, neither pastoral councils nor lay apostolate councils are to limit the autonomy of the laity.

17. Apart from the "pastoral plan," the examples in the Directory of what the bishop may consult about are drawn from the 1973 Circular Letter *Omnes Christifideles* by the Congregation for the Clergy, par 9: "The pastoral council, therefore, can give the bishop great help by presenting him with proposals and suggestions—regarding missionary, catechetical and apostolic undertakings within the diocese; concerning the promotion of doctrinal formation and the sacramental life of the faithful; concerning pastoral activities to help the priests in the various social and territorial areas of the diocese; concerning public opinion on matters pertaining to the Church as it is more likely to be fostered in the present time; etc." *Omnes Christifideles* was discussed in chap. 10 above, "What Pastoral Means."

18. "Faith, orthodoxy, moral principles or laws of the universal Church" is a quotation from the Congregation for the Clergy, Circular Letter (*Omnes Christifideles*, par. 9). Some dioceses add to the list of what is beyond the competence of the pastoral council, stating (for example) that pastoral councils cannot treat questions about administration (see chap. 10, n. 21). Such an addition to the list goes beyond the intention of the Congregation.

19. This quotation from par. 184 of the 2004 Directory (*Apostolorum successores*) echoes the 1973 Directory (*Ecclesia imago*). There we read that "By its study and reflection, the council furnishes the judgments necessary to enable the diocesan community to plan its pastoral program systematically and to fulfill it effectively" (par. 204). This is one of the earliest references in official Church documents to pastoral planning.

20. The passage contains a reference to c. 513, §2: "When the see is vacant the pastoral council ceases to exist."

21. This was implicit in a record of one conversation leading to the publication of the revised Code of Canon Law in the Roman journal entitled *Communicationes*. There, canon law experts asked whether the 1965 Decree on the Laity (no. 26) and the 1973 Directory on Bishops (no. 179)

are indeed sources for "parish" councils, and how the word *pastoral* limits the council's competence. "Dall'esame delle osservazioni generali si traggono le seguenti conclusioni: 1) È opportune parlare del Consiglio pastorale parrocchiale (*Decr. Apostolicam actuositatem*, nn. 1 e 26 e *Direttorio per i Vescovi*, no. 179)? Un Consultore suggerisce che venga chiamato «Consiglio parrocchiale», ma, secondo Mons. Segretario ed altri, sembra preferibile aggiungere l'aggetivo «pastorale» per circoscrivere la sua competenza, che non si estende al regime, all'amministrazione dei beni, ecc." (19 April 1980, meeting of the Coetus studiorum de populo Dei, *Communicationes* 13 [1981], 146).

22. In *Ad gentes divinitus* (Decree on the Church's Missionary Activity), missionary bishops are encouraged to establish pastoral councils to "coordinate" their diocesan apostolate. The verb *to coordinate* is more commonly associated with lay apostolate council. There we read: "It is the responsibility of the bishop, as the head of the diocesan apostolate and its center of unity, to promote missionary activity, guide and coordinate it, so that the spontaneous zeal of those who engage in this work may be safeguarded and fostered....For better coordination, the bishop should, as far as possible, establish a pastoral council in which clergy, religious and lay people would have a part through elected delegates." (*Ad gentes divinitus*, in *Vatican Council II*, ed. Austin Flannery, vol. 1 *The Conciliar and Post-Conciliar Documents*, no. 30, 847).

23. The 1973 Directory on Bishops (*Ecclesiae imago*) spoke (in par. 179) about parish *pastoral* councils that undertake the lay apostolate. "As regards effective organization for the work of caring for souls, besides the broader guidelines mentioned above (cf. n. 176) the bishop shall consider that kind of parish best...in which laymen, according to the office given them, take part in the parish pastoral council and take charge of works of the apostolate proper to themselves" (n. 179, 92).

CHAPTER 14

How to Make a Council More Pastoral

In the introduction, we said that this book would resolve two disputed questions about pastoral councils. The first question was about the origin of the pastoral council. That origin, we saw, is not to be found in the Vatican II Decree on the Laity. Although paragraph 26 of the Decree is often cited as a source, it does not speak about "pastoral" councils, but instead about councils to promote the lay apostolate. The origin of the parish pastoral council is actually in Vatican II's Decree on Bishops. Paragraph 27 recommended pastoral councils at the diocesan level to serve the apostolate of pastors. These councils were first recommended at the parish level in the 1973 Circular Letter by the Congregation for the Clergy, and written into canon 536 of the Code of Canon Law. The origin of the pastoral council is not the Laity Decree but the Bishops Decree.

As to the second disputed question about the purpose of councils, we have a definitive answer based on ample documentation. The pastoral council does not focus on the lay apostolate. It does not make policy on its own initiative. It does not exist to coordinate ministerial committees or commissions. No, it serves the apostolate of pastor. It aids him in the exercise his ministry of parish leadership. It helps by investigating under his direction some aspect of the parish reality, reflecting on it, and recommending to him its conclusions. He consults it, in short, to do pastoral planning.

If the truly pastoral council serves the pastor's apostolate by helping him plan for the parish, how can we make councils more pastoral? The first step is to help Catholics understand consultation in the Church. The Church does not recommend that pastors establish councils to ease their workload and delegate to the laity what they are not able to do themselves. Nor does it propose councils as a way of managing the parish or coordinating ministries. No, it promotes councils because it wants pastors to make wise decisions. It wants pastors to draw upon the good sense of parishioners so that decisions are prudent and adapted well to the community's needs. Both pastors and councillors need to understand their distinctive roles as defined by the Church's official documents.

After the council has recommended its conclusions, the pastor may implement them using parish staff members or volunteers. He may even call upon council members to help. But strictly speaking, implementation belongs to him, not to them. The pastoral council is not an executive body that carries out plans under its own initiative. It does not coordinate parish organizations on its own authority. It is rather a consultative body that serves the pastor's apostolate by dedicating itself to pastoral planning with him. In order to make councils more pastoral, council members must understand consultation as the Church understands it. The pastor consults his councillors. They serve by investigating, reflecting, and recommending conclusions. When they do their work well, the pastor will accept their recommendations and implement them.

A PASTORAL COUNCIL FOUNDATION DOCUMENT

In practical terms, councils can become more pastoral by reviewing their bylaws or foundational documents. In that way they can ensure that the documents reflect the Church's teaching. To that end, consider the following parish pastoral council "foundation document." The document is brief and it reflects the Church's teaching about the pastoral council.

1. Introduction

Recognizing that sound pastoral decisions are informed by the wisdom of the People of God, Father _____ established the pastoral council of _____ Church on [date]. The documents of the Second Vatican Council recommended the establishment of such councils. They state that Catholics share in the apostolate of the pastor. By establishing a pastoral council, the pastor acknowledges the wisdom of his parishioners and expresses his desire to share with them his responsibility for the governance of the parish.

This opening paragraph expresses the distinctly pastoral nature of the council. It exists to help the pastor exercise his ministry of parish leadership. This reflects the teaching of Vatican II's Decree on Bishops and subsequent official documents. The members have a share in the ministry of pastor. They do not replace that ministry, but they augment it with the wisdom that belongs to the community. They enable the pastor to make prudent decisions. They enable him to be a Good Shepherd who knows what is best for his people because he has consulted them.

2. Purpose

The purpose of the parish pastoral council is to investigate pastoral matters, to consider them thoroughly, and to propose practical conclusions about them. The council's task is, first of all, to study those matters brought to its attention and shed light on them. Its second task is to reflect on them thoroughly, to discern their true nature, to evaluate and to ponder them. Its final task is to draw sound conclusions. The council presents these conclusions to the pastor in the form of recommendations. This threefold task of the council—investigating, considering, and recommending conclusions—is called pastoral planning. After the pastor has accepted the recommendations of the council, he directs their implementation. Council members may assist him, but strictly speaking, implementation is the responsibility of the pastor, not the council.

The definition of the council's purpose is almost a direct quotation from the Decree on Bishops (par. 27). It has been reaffirmed in most other Vatican documents pertaining to pastoral councils. Pastors consult councils by asking them to investigate, reflect, and recommend. The implementation of these recommendations does not belong to the pastoral council on its own. The pastor must first accept them. The council has a consultative-only vote. It cannot legislate for the parish. The Church does not want to force pastors to take poor advice. But once the pastor has accepted the council's recommendations, he can implement them with the help of the parish staff and volunteers. After that, he can invite the council to study how effectively the recommendations have been implemented.

3. Scope

The scope of the council embraces all the matters about which the pastor consults it. These may include everything that pertains to the pastor's ministries of proclaiming God's word, celebrating the sacraments, caring for the faithful, promoting the mission of the Church to the world, and being a good steward of parish resources. The scope includes all the practical matters of parish life. There is, in short, nothing about which the pastor may not consult the council, apart from faith, orthodoxy, moral principles or laws of the universal Church.

The Church teaches that pastors may consult about any practical matter. It does not oblige them to consult about this matter or that. It implies that the pastor knows what he needs to consult about. Nor does the Church exclude any practical matter, warning that there are practical matters (e.g., administration or finance) about which the pastor may not consult. Once again, the council exists to serve his apostolate of pastoral leadership. The good pastor knows that he does not know everything. He consults so that he may benefit from the wisdom of his people. He should indicate to the council what he is consulting about, how long he expects the consultation to last, and what he hopes for in terms of a final product, such as a report, a plan, or a policy.

4. Criteria for Membership

Pastoral council members are chosen, above all, for their ability to accomplish the main task of the council—the work of investigating, considering, and recommending practical conclusions. They are baptized Catholics, in good standing with the Church, who reflect the parish's various neighborhoods, social and professional groups, and apostolates.

> Finally, they are parishioners noted for their faith, good
> morals, and prudence.

The primary criterion for council membership is that the prospective councillor is able to do what every councillor is expected to do. He or she is to serve the pastor's apostolate by engaging in the work of pastoral planning. When the pastor consults the council, the members must be able to put their gifts as planners—their gifts of study, reflection, and deliberation—at the service of the Church to which they belong and are committed. The Church seeks councillors who are wise and prudent. Their lives should reflect that wisdom and prudence.

5. Selection of Members

> Twelve pastoral council members are elected every three
> years. The election takes place at an assembly during the
> month of September to which all parishioners are invited.
> The assembly introduces parishioners to the work of the
> pastoral council. The pastor explains his motives for establishing it and invites parishioners to express their hopes
> for it. Then the participants at the assembly identify the
> strengths of the parish and those areas in which the council may help it to develop. The pastor invites a reflection
> on the qualities of a good councillor and invites nominations. Then, participants elect, in an atmosphere of prayer
> and discernment, the twelve new councillors.

This section of the foundation document is unusual in that it departs from the staggered elections that are the norm in the United States. Instead, it recommends the selection of twelve councillors at an open meeting once every three years. This is akin to the process described in chapter 6. Councillors serve for three years and then depart from the council. The parish acknowledges their work and new councillors are chosen at an open meeting. Many parish council guidelines recommend staggered elections (in which new people join the council every year) by saying that such a process guarantees continuity. They say that veteran councillors can help form the new members. But it may be worthwhile for the pastor to consult with an entirely new group every three years. He can turn its attention to new topics that were never considered by previous councils.

6. Officers

The pastor presides at every meeting of the council. He consults, he accepts or rejects recommendations, and he develops the agenda with the council officers. The pastor and councillors select three officers from among their number. They are the chairperson, vice-chairperson, and secretary. With the pastor they develop the council agenda. The chairperson facilitates council discussions, making sure that everyone speaks and is heard. The chairperson also monitors the work of the councillors between regular meetings. The vice-chairperson assists the chairperson and facilitates meetings in the chairperson's absence. The secretary keeps the minutes. He or she ensures that they are sent, along with the agenda and supporting documents, to each councillor at least one week before every meeting.

The pastor presides at the council because he is doing the consulting. He relies upon a chairperson but not a "president." The chairperson and vice-chairperson have the duty of *facilitating*—that is, making the council meetings easy and comfortable. They ensure that everyone has a chance to speak and be heard. The secretary keeps a record of the meeting that is confidential but not secret. In other words, the minutes of the meeting are a public document that conveys the truth of the meeting, but never seeks to embarrass the people present at it. The minutes are important to the development of the agenda, which will be discussed below.

7. Operation

The pastoral council has a three-year planning cycle, and members are selected for a three-year term. The pastor defines the theme of the planning cycle during the September assembly at which the council is selected. In the beginning of the council's second and third year, the members facilitate a parish assembly to report on the council's progress and to elicit the advice of parishioners. At the end of the third year, the council completes its work, a new council is selected, and a new planning cycle begins.

This item in the foundation document is also unusual. It envisions a pastoral council that serves a three-year term. The term has a general focus. The pastor states what he wants to consult about (e.g., hospitality, ecumenism, stewardship, intercultural cooperation, evangelization, etc.). He attracts people to the council who have a particular interest in its general focus and learn about it through parish assemblies. By describing the focus publicly, the pastor awakens interest in the topic and attracts new councillors. The three-year term and the general focus are unusual because many councils do not do long-range planning.

8. Agenda

The pastor develops the agenda with the council officers. It states the goals for each meeting, the means and group process for reaching the goals, and the materials needed to accomplish them. The agenda guides the meeting. It begins with a review of the minutes of the previous meeting and concludes with a brief evaluation. If the pastor is dissatisfied with the consultation, he expresses his reservations and asks the council to clarify whatever remains obscure. When he is satisfied with the consultation, he formally accepts the council's recommendations. He may then ask the parish staff or other parishioners to implement them.

The development of the council agenda is the most important preparation for every council meeting. By developing an agenda, the pastor and the officers judge what matters will come before the council, and what matters do not deserve the council's attention at a given time. The pastor and officers should also state in the agenda what they expect the council to do (e.g., to hear a report, to brainstorm, to discuss a book or article, to plan a group process, to put concerns into an order of priority, to pray over a decision, etc.). Because he is doing the consulting, the pastor should say what will help him best.

9. Relation to the Staff and Finance Council

The pastor consults others besides the pastoral council about parish governance. He relies upon the parish staff for their expertise and consults them daily about the management of parish operations. Indeed, he may occasionally ask parish staff members to attend council meetings in order to put their knowledge at the service of the pastoral council. Moreover, the pastor relies on the finance council to develop, monitor, and report on the parish budget. Finance council members are chosen for their technical skill in realms of accounting and finance. The pastoral council, by contrast, offers practical wisdom. That is the ability to investigate pastoral matters in a general way, to reflect on them deeply in dialogue, and to propose conclusions appropriate to the parish.

The difference between technical knowledge and practical wisdom, described in chapter 5, is essential. Without it we cannot clearly distinguish between the pastoral council and the finance council or parish staff. Pastoral councils seek wisdom by deliberating about and planning for the parish's common good. Finance councils and expert staff members apply the technical knowledge of their disciplines to specific issues that parishes face. Pastors should ask those with special knowledge about matters that pertain to their technical expertise. They should ask pastoral council members about matters that do not depend on expert opinion but on the wisdom of a course of action that will have consequences for the entire community.

10. Meetings

The pastoral council meets once a month from September to May. Meetings are two hours in length. Between the monthly meetings, council members are expected to follow up the previous meeting and prepare for the next. This usually entails work on *ad hoc* committees. The first meeting of the new pastoral council is dedicated to the call and mission of the newly-chosen members. During the final meeting of each year, the councillors reflect on the progress of the three-year planning cycle. They assess their progress toward reaching the council's goals.

Most councils meet on a monthly basis. The best meetings are those for which the council has a clear agenda. From the agenda, members should be able to see how the upcoming meeting builds upon the results of the last meeting. The agenda should also clarify how the work of the upcoming meeting fits into the council's overall process of planning. If the final result of the planning process is a written report, for example, the agenda should sketch what the councillors still need to accomplish. It should indicate how people need to prepare for the meeting and enable the chairperson to pace the meeting comfortably.

CONSULTATION AS THE CHURCH SEES IT

The Church's official teaching views pastoral councils as a participation in the apostolate of the pastor. To him the bishop has entrusted the parish. He is to be a good shepherd. The Gospel of John expresses his ministry in traditional imagery. "He calls his own sheep by name." "They know his voice." He comes "that they may have life and have it abundantly." The good shepherd can say, "I know my own and my own know me." In other words, the gospel portrays the shepherd and the sheep as intimates. They know each other. He serves them as a leader who brings them life. He knows what gives life because he has consulted his people.

Consultation should never be understood as if the pastor were indifferent to it. Rather, he consults his people because he wants to know them. This means, of course, that he seeks to know them as individuals. But it means more than that. He desires to share their wisdom. He believes that God's Spirit dwells in them. He strives to hear God's Word as expressed in their labor of study and reflection. He can only be a good shepherd if his decisions on the parish's behalf are wise. That is why he consults. By asking his people to help him make sound decisions, he expresses his trust in them and his faith in God.

At the most profound level, councils can become more pastoral when pastors give them a real share in their ministry of governance. As we saw in chapter 7, the Church's official documents affirm the belief that all Christians are configured to Christ. Depending on their gifts, they can as councillors enhance the apostolate of the pastor, who heads the parish as Christ heads the Church. He can make his council more pastoral by making the Church's intention about consultation his own. This happens whenever he consults in earnest. It happens whenever he asks important questions and demands well-researched and discerning answers. It happens whenever he expects the council to exercise its office of investigating, reflecting, and recommending. When pastors consult seriously, and when members genuinely put their gifts at the service of the Church, councils become ever more pastoral.

Appendix
Pastoral Councils Online

Once published, a book never changes. The book in your hands will always mirror the author's point of view in 2010, the year it was published. A Web site, however, can be updated continuously. On my pastoral council Web site, PastoralCouncils.com, you can read news about parish pastoral councils, learn about changes in the way the Church interprets parish pastoral councils, and post your own comments.

The most up-to-date page on the Web site is called "Discussion," and you can access it by clicking on the menu bar. The discussion page chronicles recent issues, debates, and contributions to the field of pastoral councils.

RECENT PUBLICATIONS

Let me give you an example. In the spring of 2010, three new books appeared, all dealing with pastoral councils:

- Dan R. Ebener, *Servant Leadership Models for Your Parish* (Paulist Press)
- Sr. Brenda L. Hermann and Msgr. James T. Gaston, *Build a Life-Giving Parish: The Gift of Counsel in the Modern World* (Ligouri Press)
- Charles E. Zech, Mary L. Gautier, Robert J. Miller, and Mary E. Bendyna, RSM, *Best Practices of Catholic Pastoral and Finance Councils* (Our Sunday Visitor Publishing Division)

These books came out in time for me to read them and briefly refer to them in the present book. But on PastoralCouncils.com, I was able to review them at length and post comments about them. Visitors to the site have only to click on the tab "What's New" in order to go to the "Past Discussion" page on the Web site, which includes the three reviews.

New books inevitably reflect old issues. This is obviously the case with the first of the three books mentioned above, Dan Ebener's *Servant Leadership Models*. The title echoes Robert K. Greenleaf's book from 1977, *Servant Leadership: A Journey into the Nature of Legitimate Power and Greatness*. Taking his cue from Greenleaf, Ebener champions those pastors who serve their congregations by helping them reach their own goal of union with God. Ebener presupposes that congregations know their goals and need help from the pastor to achieve them. My review raised a question about servant leadership in an unusual case: What happens when a pastor doubts the congregation's understanding of its goal? What happens when the pastor gets caught between the different and contradictory expectations of the congregation and those of the bishop? The online review pursues this question.

The second book, *Build a Life-Giving Parish*, expresses an important concern about the role of pastoral planning by councils. The authors, Brenda Hermann and James Gaston, doubt that councils ought to be pastoral planners. They prefer that councils not dedicate themselves to setting goals and objectives. They should not concern themselves with evaluating the parish's progress in meeting them. Instead, the authors recommend that councils discern God's will, bringing the concerns of the laity and the ministry of the pastor into dialogue with one another. The book reflects a dissatisfaction with pastoral planning, which I (contrary to the authors) take to be the primary purpose of councils. My own book lacks the space to adequately respond to the thesis of Hermann and Gaston, but the review on PastoralCouncils.com replies more fully.

The third book from 2010, *Best Practices of Catholic Pastoral and Finance Councils*, is the most important. Based on a response by 661 parishes to surveys administered in 2007, the book draws general conclusions about how councils understand themselves. It marks an advance beyond my own method, which generalizes about councils after reviewing guidelines published by dioceses. Actual survey data from 661 parishes offers a comprehensive and accurate portrait of councils. The review of *Best Practices of Catholic Pastoral and Finance Councils* on PastoralCouncils.com enables people to learn about an up-to-date survey of U.S. councils.

NEW COUNCILLORS

In addition to providing reviews of current council publications, the Web site can be used to teach new pastoral council members. The initial page of PastoralCouncils.com provides links to PowerPoint presentations, including an introduction to the PPC, an overview of PPC functions, and a sketch of planning by the PPC. Councillors can download and view these presentations at home, or pastors can themselves download and present them using their own computer and projector. In addition, there is a free online Introductory Course that viewers can access from the initial page of PastoralCouncils.com. The course includes audiovisual lectures, reading materials, and even quizzes. Councillors can take the course in the privacy of their homes, then come to the council meeting and discuss what they have learned.

BIBLIOGRAPHIES

PastoralCouncils.com also allows access to a number of guidelines and manuals for parish pastoral and finance councils posted by dioceses on the Internet. The Web site's *Bibliography* page leads the reader to a further page, *Diocesan Guidelines*, which has links to diocesan publications throughout the United States. The *Bibliography* page also leads the reader to a page entitled *Vatican Documents*. There one can find all the relevant passages about councils in official Church publications since 1965.

OTHER LINKS

Most of the information on PastoralCouncils.com appears under five headings on the menu bar:

- Parish Pastoral Councils Today
- Planning

- Management
- Spirituality
- Consultation

The articles and documents that appear under these headings lead pastors and council members into wide-ranging discussions about the how and why of pastoral councils.

A sixth tab on the menu bar, *Consejos*, introduces Spanish-speaking readers to the "normas" for pastoral councils published by the Archdiocese of Los Angeles. It also offers Spanish-language presentations about consultation and establishing effective councils.

Notes Index

References are listed by endnote beginning with the chapter indicated.

Bibliography

Ahlin, Robert J. "Parish Councils: A Theological and Canonical Foundation." JCD diss., The Catholic University of America, 1982.

Anchorage, Archdiocese of. *Pastoral Council Manual: A Call to Discern as Disciples.* Approved by Most Rev. Roger L. Schwietz, OMI, June 24, 2005. Anchorage, AK: Office of Evangelization, Archdiocese of Anchorage, 2005. Available online at https://alatar.nocdirect.com/~jarchdio/documents/PastoralCouncilManual_000.pdf (accessed February 5, 2009).

Aristotle. *Nicomachean Ethics.* Translated by Martin Ostwald. Indianapolis, IN: Bobbs-Merrill, 1962.

Baker, Thomas, and Frank Ferrone. *Liturgy Committee Basics: A No-Nonsense Guide.* Washington, DC: Pastoral Press, 1985.

Baltimore, Archdiocese of. *Building One Body in Christ: The Ministry of the Parish Pastoral Council.* With a letter from William Cardinal Keeler, Archbishop of Baltimore. Baltimore: Archdiocese of Baltimore, 1997.

Bannon, William J., and Suzanne Donovan. *Volunteers and Ministry: A Manual for Developing Parish Volunteers.* New York and Ramsey, NJ: Paulist Press, 1983.

Bausch, William J. *The Hands-On Parish.* Mystic, CT: Twenty-Third Publications, 1989.

Beal, John P., James A. Coriden, and Thomas J. Green, eds. *New Commentary on the Code of Canon Law.* New York and Mahwah, NJ: Paulist Press, 2000.

Broderick, Robert C. *Parish Council Handbook: A Handbook to Bring the Power of Renewal to Your Parish.* Chicago: Franciscan Herald Press, 1968.

Caparros, Ernest, Michel Thériault, Jean Thorn, eds. *Code of Canon Law Annotated.* Montreal: Wilson and Lafleur, 1993.

Castelli, Jim, and Joseph Gremillion. *The Emerging Parish: The Notre Dame Study of Catholic Life Since Vatican II.* San Francisco: Harper & Row, 1987. See Leege and Gremillion.

Champlin, Joseph. "Ten Guiding Principles of Parish Councils." Written in consultation with the Presbyteral Council of the Diocese of St. Augustine. St. Augustine, FL: Office of the Chancery, 1985.

Charlotte, Diocese of (2007). See Jugis, Peter.

Charlotte, Diocese of (1999). *Parish Pastoral Council and Commissions Manual.* Prepared by the Office of Planning for Most. Rev. William G. Curlin, December 8, 1999. Available at http://www. charlottediocese.org/parish.html (accessed April 27, 2007). The Charlotte manual was completely revised in 2007.

Cleveland, Diocese of. *Parish Finance Council Policy.* Cleveland, OH: Diocese of Cleveland, 1991.

Coetus studiorum de populo Dei. Report on the meeting of April 19, 1980. *Communicationes* 13 (1981): 146.

Cooperrider, David L.; Peter F. Sorensen, Jr.; Diana Whitney; and Therese F. Yaeger, eds. *Appreciative Inquiry: Rethinking the Organization Toward a Positive Theory of Change.* Champaign, IL: Stipes Publishing, 2000.

Cooperrider, David L., Suresh Srivastva and associates. *Appreciative Management and Leadership.* San Francisco: Jossey-Bass, 1990.

Cunningham, Richard C. "The Laity in the Revised Code." In *Code, Community, Ministry: Selected Studies for the Parish Minister Introducing the Revised Code of Canon Law,* edited by James H. Provost, 32–37. Washington, DC: Canon Law Society of America, 1983.

Dalton, William. "Parish Councils or Parish Pastoral Councils?" *Studia Canonica* 22 (1988): 169–185.

DeLambo, David. *Lay Parish Ministers: A Study of Emerging Leadership.* New York: National Pastoral Life Center, 2005.

DeLambo, David, and Richard Krivanka. "Appreciative Inquiry: A Powerful Process for Parish Listening and Planning." In *Four Ways to Build More Effective Parish Councils: A Pastoral Approach,* edited by Mark F. Fischer and Mary Margaret Raley, 87–101. Mystic, CT: Twenty-Third Publications, 2002.

Des Moines, Diocese of. *Pastoral Councils* (2001). The ad hoc Pastoral Council Planning Committee that formed the original document included: Mrs. Candy Chambers, Rev. David Fleming, Dr. Luvern Gubbels, Rev. Wayne Gubbels, Mrs. Cindee Hays, Rev. Gene Koch, Mrs. Shirley Koeppel, and Rev. Paul Monahan. The Introduction stated that "This final document has been accepted for implementation by Bishop [Joseph L.] Charron for the formation of the Diocese of Des Moines Pastoral Council. Over time, these new Pastoral Council Principles and Guidelines will direct the restoration and/or renewal of both diocesan and parish pastoral councils" (p. 1). Available at http://www.dmdiocese.org/files/documents/422_pastoral%20council%20guidelines.pdf (accessed February 5, 2009).

Doyle, Michael, and David Straus. *How to Make Meetings Work: The New Interactive Method.* New York: Jove Books, 1983.

Doyle, Ruth T., Robert E. Schmitz, and Mary Beth Celio, eds. *Laity, Parish and Ministry.* Monograph no. 1 in Research Monographs of the Catholic Research Forum of the Conference for Pastoral Planning and Council Development. New York: Office of Pastoral Research and Planning, Archdiocese of New York, 1999.

Dubuque, Archdiocese of. "Manual for Parish Councils" (unfinished draft, April 3, 2007). It includes a three-page "Annual Planning Process" (4–6).

Ebener, Dan R. *Servant Leadeship Models for Your Parish.* New York and Mahwah, NJ: Paulist Press, 2010.

Fargo, Diocese of. *Diocesan Pastoral Council Handbook* (including maps dated June 30, 2005). In e-mail message to author from Very Rev. Brian Moen, Chancellor, January 29, 2007.

Ferguson, Jane. *A Handbook for Parish Pastoral Councils.* Dublin: Columba Press, 2005.

Fischer, Mark F. "Breathe Fresh Spirit into Your Parish Pastoral Council." *Today's Parish* (January 1997): 29–31.

———. "Parish Councils: Where Does the Pastor Fit In?" *Today's Parish* 23:7 (November/December 1991): 13–15.

———. "Parish Pastoral Councils: How Many Are There? How Do Bishops Support Them?" In *Laity, Parish and Ministry,* edited by Ruth T. Doyle, Robert E. Schmitz, and Mary Beth Celio,

82–106. New York: Office of Pastoral Research and Planning, Archdiocese of New York, 1999.

———. "Parish Pastoral Councils: Purpose, Consultation, Leadership." *Center Papers*, no. 4. New York: National Pastoral Life Center, 1990.

———. "The Pastor, the Experts, and the Pastoral Council." *Today's Parish* 34:3 (March 2002): 12–15.

———. *Pastoral Councils in Today's Catholic Parish*. Mystic, CT: Twenty-Third Publications, 2001. The book, now out of print, is available as a free download at http://www.mfischer.stjohnsem.edu/.

———. "Should Finance Councils Answer to Parish Councils?" *Today's Parish* (March 1994): 21–23, 32.

———. "What was Vatican II's Intent Regarding Parish Councils?" *Studia Canonica* 33 (1999): 5–25. Available at http://www.pastoralcouncils.com/A56.htm.

Fischer, Mark F., and Mary Margaret Raley, eds. *Four Ways to Build More Effective Parish Councils: A Pastoral Approach*. Mystic, CT: Twenty-Third Publications, 2002.

Fischer, Mark F., and Sr. Rosalie Murphy, SNDdeN., "Selecting Effective Pastoral Council Members" (2004). Available at http://www.usccb.org/laity/pastoral.shtml.

Flaherty, John P., ed. *Diocesan Efforts at Parish Reorganization*. Clearwater, FL: Conference for Pastoral Planning and Council Development (CPPCD), 1995.

Flaherty, John. "Planning: Idol or Icon of Pastoral Councils?" In *Four Ways to Build More Effective Parish Councils: A Pastoral Approach*, edited by Mark F. Fischer and Mary Margaret Raley, 119–136. Mystic, CT: Twenty-Third Publications, 2002.

Fleischer, Barbara J. *Facilitating for Growth: A Guide for Scripture Groups and Small Christian Communities*. Collegeville, MN: Liturgical Press, 1993.

Froehle, Bryan T., and Mary L. Gautier. *Catholicism USA: A Portrait of the Catholic Church in the United States*. Maryknoll, NY: Orbis Books, 2000.

———. *National Parish Inventory Project Report*. Washington, DC: Center for Applied Research in the Apostolate at Georgetown University, October, 1999.

Gaylord, Diocese of. *Parish Pastoral/Finance Council Guidelines.* Approved by Bishop Patrick R. Cooney. Revised November 2005. Available at http://www.dioceseofgaylord.org/inside/parish-pastoral-and-finance-council-guidelines-249/ (accessed April 27, 2007).

Great Falls–Billings, Diocese of. *Parish Pastoral Council Guidelines.* Approved by Most. Rev. Anthony M. Milone, May 26, 1996. Available at http://www.dioceseofgfb.org/Diocesan_%20Policies/parish_pastoral_council_guidelin.htm (accessed February 2, 2007).

Green, Thomas J. "Critical Reflections on the Schema on the People of God." *Studia Canonica* 14 (1980): 235–314.

Green Bay, Diocese of. *That All May Be One: Norms for Parish Pastoral Councils.* With a letter from Bishop Adam J. Maida. Prepared by Rev. Larry Canavera and Sr. Luanne Smits, SSND. Green Bay, WI: Office of Parish Services, 1986.

Gremillion, Joseph, and Jim Castelli. *The Emerging Parish: The Notre Dame Study of Catholic Life since Vatican II.* San Francisco: Harper & Row, 1987. See Leege and Gremillion.

Griese, Orville. "The New Code of Canon Law and Parish Councils." *Homiletic and Pastoral Review* 85:4 (January 1985): 47–53.

———. "Pastor-Parish Council Collaboration." *The Priest* 33:2 (February 1977): 19–22, 24.

Gubish, Mary Ann, and Susan Jenny, SC, with Arlene McGannon. *Revisioning the Parish Pastoral Council: A Workbook.* New York and Mahwah, NJ: Paulist Press, 2001.

Harrisburg, Diocese of. *Council Policy and Guidelines.* Harrisburg, PA: Diocese of Harrisburg, 1985.

Heaps, John. *Parish Pastoral Councils: Co-responsibility and Leadership.* Ridgefield, CT: Morehouse, 1993.

Hermann, Brenda L., and James T. Gaston. *Build a Life-Giving Parish: The Gift of Counsel in the Modern World.* Ligouri, MO: Ligouri Publications, 2010.

Hinze, Bradford E. *Practices of Dialogue in the Roman Catholic Church: Aims and Obstacles, Lessons and Laments.* New York: Continuum, 2006.

Howes, Robert G. *Creating an Effective Parish Pastoral Council.* Collegeville, MN: Liturgical Press, 1991.

————. *Parish Planning: A Practical Guide to Shared Responsibility.* Collegeville, MN: Liturgical Press, 1994.

John Paul II. *Christifideles Laici* (The Vocation and the Mission of the Lay Faithful in the Church and in the World). Post-Synodal Apostolic Exhortation. Rome: January 30, 1987. In *Origins* 18:35 (February 9, 1989): 561, 563–595.

————. *Ecclesia de mysterio* (Instruction on Certain Questions Regarding Collaboration of the Non-Ordained Faithful in the Sacred Ministry of Priest). See Sacred Congregation for the Clergy, et al.

————. *Ecclesia in Asia* (The Church in Asia). Apostolic Exhortation. New Delhi: November 6, 1999. Available at http://www. vatican.va/holy_father/john_paul_ii/apost_exhortations/ documents/hf_jp-ii_exh_06111999_ecclesia-in-asia_en.html. (accessed November 2, 2007).

————. *Novo millennio ineunte* (At the Beginning of the New Millennium). Apostolic Letter. Rome: January 6, 2001. Available at http://www.vatican.va/holy_father/john_paul_ii/apost_letters/ documents/hf_jp-ii_apl_20010106_novo-millennio-ineunte_ en.html (accessed September 11, 2007).

————. *Pastores dabo vobis* (I Will Give You Shepherds). Post-Synodal Apostolic Exhortation. Rome: March 25, 1992. Washington, DC: United States Catholic Conference, 1997.

Jugis, Bishop Peter. "Guiding the Roles of Pastors and Pastoral Councils." Including Appendix A: "Ministerial Responsibilities of the Commissions" (511–514) and Appendix B: "Suggested Bylaws for Pastoral Councils" (514–516). *Origins* 37:32 (January 24, 2008): 505–516. Available at: http://www.charlotte diocese.org/customers/101092709242178/filemanager/george/ Pastoral_Council_Handbook_Rev_2007_Final.pdf (accessed February 13, 2009).

Keating, John. "Consultation in the Parish." *Origins* 14:17 (October 11, 1984): 257, 259–266.

Kim Se-Mang, Peter. *Parish Councils on Mission: Coresponsibility and Authority among Pastors and Parishioners.* Kuala Lumpur: Benih Publisher, 1991.

Laz, Medard. *Making Parish Meetings Work.* Notre Dame, IN: Ave Maria Press, 1997.

Leege, David, and Joseph Gremillion, eds. *Notre Dame Study of Catholic Parish Life*. Reports 1–10. Notre Dame, IN: University of Notre Dame, 1984–1987. Ninth Report. "Parish Life Among the Leaders," by David C. Leege. Published in December, 1986 as one of ten independent reports. See Castelli and Gremillion.

Lyons, Bernard. *Parish Councils: Renewing the Christian Community*. Foreword by Bishop John J. Wright. Techny, IL: Divine Word Publications, 1967.

Lyons, Enda. *Partnership in Parish: A Vision for Parish Life, Mission, and Ministry*. Dublin: Columba Press, 1987.

Mahony, Roger, and the People of God of the Archdiocese of Los Angeles. *Gathered and Sent: Documents of the Synod of the Archdiocese of Los Angeles 2003*, bilingual (English/Spanish) edition. Edited by Kris Fankhouser et al. Chicago: Liturgy Training Publications, 2003.

Marceaux, Sidney J. "The Pastoral Council." JCD diss., Pontifical University of Studies at St. Thomas Aquinas in the City, Rome, 1980.

McKinney, Mary Benet. *Sharing Wisdom: A Process for Group Decision Making*. Allen, TX: Tabor Publishing, 1987. Reprint, Chicago: Thomas More Press, 1998.

Mealey, Mark S. "The Parish Pastoral Council in the United States of America: Applications of Canon 536." JCD diss., St. Paul University, Ottawa, 1989.

Miller, Robert J. "Inter-Parochial Pastoral Councils: An Emerging Model for Parish Consultative Bodies." Paper sponsored by the Conference for Pastoral Planning and Council Development and by the National Federation of Priests' Councils as part of the Emerging Models of Pastoral Leadership. Archdiocese of Philadelphia: Office for Research and Planning, 2007.

Milwaukee, Archdiocese of. *Living the Spirit: A Parish Council Manual*. 4th ed. Edited by Denise Pheifer. Archdiocese of Milwaukee: Office for Parish Stewardship and Lay Leadership Development, 1991.

———. *Parish Committee Ministry*. Milwaukee: Archdiocese of Milwaukee, 1991.

Nashville, Diocese of. *Parish Pastoral Council Handbook*. Prepared by Ministry Formation Services (Joceline Lemaire). Approved by

Most. Rev. Edward U. Kmiec, January 15, 2004. Available at http://www.dioceseofnashville.com/parishpastcouncil.htm (accessed April 27, 2007).

National Conference of Catholic Bishops, Committee on Budget and Finance. "Diocesan Internal Controls: A Framework." Washington, DC: U.S. Catholic Conference, 1995. Available at http://www.usccb.org/finance/internal.shtml.

Newsome, Robert R. *The Ministering Parish: Methods and Procedures for Pastoral Organization.* New York and Ramsey. NJ: Paulist Press, 1982.

Norwich, Diocese of. *Guidelines for Parish Pastoral Councils.* Approved by Most. Rev. Daniel A. Hart. Norwich: Diocese of Norwich, 2001. Available at http://www.norwichdiocese.org/Documents. htm (accessed April 27, 2007).

Ochoa, Xaverius, ed. *Leges Ecclesiae post Codicem iuris canonici editae.* Institutem Iuridicum Claretianum. 8 vols. Vatican City: Libreria Editrice Vaticana; and Rome: Commentarium Pro Religiosis, 1973–1998.

O'Connor, James I., ed. "Officially Published Documents Affecting the Code of Canon Law 1973–1977." *Canon Law Digest* 8 (1978).

The Official Catholic Directory: 2006. Providence, NJ: P. J. Kenedy and Sons, 2006.

Olsen, Charles M. *Transforming Church Boards into Communities of Spiritual Leaders.* New York: Alban Institute, 1995.

Paddock, Susan Star. *Appreciative Inquiry in the Catholic Church.* Plano, TX: Thin Book Publishing, 2003.

Pagé, Roch. *The Diocesan Pastoral Council.* Translated by Bernard A. Prince. Paramus, NJ: Newman Press, 1970.

Parise, Michael. "Forming Your Parish Pastoral Council." *The Priest* 51:7 (July 1995): 43–47.

Paul VI. *Ecclesiae Sanctae I* (Apostolic Letter on the Implementation of the Decrees *Christus Dominus, Presbyterorum Ordinis,* and *Perfectae Caritatis*). Rome: August 6, 1966. Translated by Austin P. Flannery. In *Vatican Council II.* Vol. 1, *The Conciliar and Post-Conciliar Documents.* Edited by Austin P. Flannery. Northport, NY: Costello Publishing Company, 1998.

———. *Encyclical of Pope Paul VI Ecclesiam Suam: The Paths of the Church*. With a Commentary by Gregory Baum, OSA. Study Club Edition. Glen Rock, NJ: Paulist Press, 1964.

Pickett, William L. *A Concise Guide to Pastoral Planning*. Notre Dame, IN: Ave Maria Press, 2007).

Plato. *Apology*. Translated by Hugh Tredennick. In *Plato: The Collected Dialogues*, Edited by Edith Hamilton and Huntington Cairns. Bollingen Series 71. Princeton, NJ: Princeton University Press, 1963.

Provost, James H. "Canon Law and the Role of Consultation." *Origins* 18:47 (May 4, 1989): 793, 795–799.

Pueblo, Diocese of. *A Handbook for Parish Pastoral Councils*. Available at http://www.dioceseofpueblo.com/Docs/Handbook%20for%20Parish%20Pastoral%20Councils.pdf (accessed April 27, 2007).

Rademacher, William J. "Parish Councils: Consultative Vote Only?" *Today's Parish* 32:3 (March 2000): 6–9.

Rademacher, William J., with Marliss Rogers. *The New Practical Guide for Parish Councils*. Foreword by Most Rev. Rembert G. Weakland, OSB. Mystic, CT: Twenty-Third Publications, 1988.

Renken, John A. "Parishes and Pastors [cc. 515–544]," In *New Commentary on the Code of Canon Law* edited by John P. Beal, James A. Coriden, and Thomas J. Green, 711. New York and Mahwah, NJ: Paulist Press, 2000.

———. "Parishes without a Resident Pastor: Comments on Canon 517, §2." In *Code, Community, Ministry: Selected Studies for the Parish Minister Introducing the Code of Canon Law*, Second Revised Edition, edited by Edward G. Pfnausch, 100–108. Washington, DC: Canon Law Society of America, 1992.

———. "Pastoral Councils: Pastoral Planning and Dialogue among the People of God." *The Jurist* 53 (1993): 132–154.

Rexhausen, Jeff, et al. *A National Study of Recent Diocesan Efforts at Parish Reorganization in the United States: Pathways for the Church of the 21st Century*. Dubuque, IA: Loras College Press, 2004.

Richmond, Diocese of. *Norms for Parish Finance Councils*. Richmond, VA: Diocese of Richmond, 1991.

Robert, Henry M. *Robert's Rules of Order*, 9th ed. Edited by Sarah Corbin Robert, with the assistance of Henry M. Robert III and William J. Evans. New York: Scott, Foresman, 1990.

Rochester, Diocese of. *Parish Pastoral Council Guidelines*. Approved by Most Rev. Matthew H. Clark, Bishop of Rochester, June 26, 2000. Available at http://www.dor.org/planning/Pastoral%20 Council%20Development/pastoralcouncil.htm (accessed April 27, 2007).

Rockford, Diocese of. *Guidelines for Parish Pastoral Councils* (September 23, 1999). Available at http://www.rockforddiocese.org/planning /PDF/PastoralCouncilNorms.pdf (accessed February 6, 2007).

Ryan, Edward E. *How to Establish a Parish Council: A Step-by-Step Program for Setting Up Parish Councils*. Chicago: Claretian, 1968.

Sacramento, Diocese of. *Parish Pastoral Council Guidelines*. Approved by Bishop William K. Weigand, November 21, 2005. Available at http://www.diocese-sacramento.org/PDFs/ParishPastoral CouncilGuidelines.pdf (accessed April 27, 2007).

Sacred Congregation for Bishops. *Apostolorum successores* (Directory for the Pastoral Ministry of Bishops). Rome: February 22, 2004. Available at http://www.vatican.va/roman_curia/congregations/ cbishops/documents/rc_con_cbishops_doc_20040222_ apostolorum-successores_en.html (accessed on September 6, 2007).

———. *Ecclesiae imago* (Directory on the Pastoral Ministry of Bishops). Rome: May 31, 1973. Translated by the Benedictine Monks of the Seminary of Christ the King in Mission, British Columbia. Ottawa: Canadian Catholic Conference, 1974.

Sacred Congregation for the Clergy. *Omnes Christifideles* (Circular Letter on "Pastoral Councils"). Published as "Patterns in Local Pastoral Councils" (*Omnes Christifideles*, January 25, 1973). *Origins* 3:12 (Sept. 13, 1973): 186–190. Also published in reference to c. 423 in James I. O'Connor, editor, *Canon Law Digest* 7: 280–288. Available at http://www.PastoralCouncils.com/ A42.htm. For the Latin text, see Sacra Congregatio Pro Clericis. *Omnes Christifideles*. Rome: January 25, 1973. In *Leges Ecclesiae post Codicem iuris canonici editae*. Edited by Xaverius Ochoa. Institutem Iuridicum Claretianum. 8 vols. Vatican City: Libreria Editrice Vaticana; and Rome: Commentarium

Pro Religiosis, 1973–1998. See vol. 5: "Leges Annis 1973–1978 Editae" (1980), col. 6444–6449.

———. *The Priest, Pastor and Leader of the Parish Community*. Rome: August 4, 2002. Available at http://www.vatican.va/roman_curia/congregations/cclergy/documents/rc_con_cclergy_doc_20020804_istruzione-presbitero_en.html (accessed on July 30, 2007).

Sacred Congregation for the Clergy and representatives from the Pontifical Council for the Laity, the Congregation for the Doctrine of the Faith, the Congregation for Divine Worship and the Discipline of the Sacraments, the Congregation for Bishops, the Congregation for the Evangelization of Peoples, the Congregation for Institutes of Consecrated Life and Societies of Apostolic Life, and the Pontifical Council for the Interpretation of Legislative Texts. *Ecclesiae de Mysterio* (Instruction on Certain Questions Regarding Collaboration of the Non-Ordained Faithful in the Sacred Ministry of Priest). Rome: August 15, 1997. Available at http://www.vatican.va/roman_curia/pontifical_councils/laity/documents/rc_con_interdic_doc_15081997_en.html (accessed on October 12, 2007).

Saint Louis, Archdiocese of. *Guidelines for the Ministry of Parish Councils*. St. Louis, MO: Archdiocese of St. Louis, 1985.

Scheets, Francis Kelly. "Parish Information Systems—Resources for Ministry." Chap. 9 in *The Parish Management Handbook: A Practical Guide for Pastors, Administrators, and Other Parish Leaders*, edited by Charles E. Zech. Mystic, CT: Twenty-Third Publications, 2003.

Scranton, Diocese of. *Directives for Parish Pastoral Councils* (September 21, 2006). Approved by Bishop Francis Martino. Available at http://www.dioceseofscranton.org/Parish%20Councils/Bishop'sLetterOnParishCouncils.asp (accessed April 27, 2007).

Seattle, Archdiocese of. *Policy and Guidelines for Parish Consultative Structures*. Archdiocese of Seattle: Planning and Research Department, 1990. Reprinted December 1993.

Sofield, Loughlan. "A Spirituality for Councils." In *Four Ways to Build More Effective Parish Councils: A Pastoral Approach*, edited by Mark F. Fischer and Mary Margaret Raley, 23–39. Mystic, CT: Twenty-Third Publications, 2002.

Sofield, Loughlan, Rosine Hammett, and Carroll Juliano. *Building Community: Christian, Caring, Vital*. Notre Dame, IN: Ave Maria Press, 1998.

Sofield, Loughlan, and Brenda Hermann. *Developing the Parish as a Community of Service*. New York: Le Jacq Publishing, 1984.

Sudbrack, Josef. "Spirituality (Part I: Concept)." 1623–29 in Karl Rahner, ed., *Sacramentum Mundi: A Concise Dictionary of Theology*. Translations edited by John Cumming. New York: Seabury, 1975.

Sweetser, Thomas, and Carol Wisniewski Holden. *Leadership in a Successful Parish*. San Francisco: Harper & Row, 1987.

Synod of Bishops (1971). *De Sacerdotio ministeriali* (The Ministerial Priesthood, November 30, 1971). Published in reference to c. 329 in *Canon Law Digest* 7: 342–366. Original text: "De Sacerdotio Ministeriali." *Acta Apostolicae Sedis* 63 (1971): 897–922.

Tighe, Marie Kevin. "Council Spirituality: Foundation for Mission." In *Developing a Vibrant Parish Pastoral Council*, ed. Arthur X. Deegan, II, 88–99. New York and Mahwah, NJ: Paulist Press, 1995.

Turley, Kathleen. "The Parish Pastoral Council and Prayer." In *Developing a Vibrant Parish Pastoral Council*, ed. Arthur X. Deegan, II, 100–106. New York and Mahwah, NJ: Paulist Press, 1995.

Vatican Council II. *Acta Synodalia Sacrosancti Concilii Oecumenici Vaticani*. 24 Volumes. Volumen I: Periodus prima, Pars I–IV; Volumen II: Periodus secunda, Pars I–VI; Volumen III: Periodus tertia, Pars I–VIII; Volumen IV: Periodus quarta, Pars I–VI. Vatican City: Typis Polyglottis Vaticanis, 1970–1978.

———. *Ad gentes divinitus* (Decree on the Church's Missionary Activity), Rome: December 7, 1965. Translated by Redmond Fitzmaurice. In *Vatican Council II*. Vol. 1, *The Conciliar and Post-Conciliar Documents*. Edited by Austin P. Flannery. Northport, NY: Costello Publishing Company, 1998.

———. *Apostolicam actuositatem* (Decree on the Apostolate of Lay People), Rome: November 18, 1965. Translated by Father Finnian, OCSO. In *Vatican Council II*. Vol. 1, *The Conciliar and*

Post-Conciliar Documents. Edited by Austin P. Flannery. Northport, NY: Costello Publishing Company, 1998.

————. *Christus Dominus* (Decree on the Pastoral Office of Bishops in the Church), Rome: October 28, 1965. Translation by Matthew Dillon, Edward O'Leary, and Austin P. Flannery. In *Vatican Council II.* Vol. 1, *The Conciliar and Post-Conciliar Documents.* Edited by Austin P. Flannery. Northport, NY: Costello Publishing Company, 1998.

————. *Lumen gentium* (Dogmatic Constitution on the Church), Rome: November. 21, 1964. Translated by Father Colman O'Neill, OP. In *Vatican Council II.* Vol. 1, *The Conciliar and Post-Conciliar Documents.* Edited by Austin P. Flannery. Northport, NY: Costello Publishing Company, 1998.

————. *Presbyterorum Ordinis* (Decree on the Ministry and Life of Priests)., Rome: December 7, 1965. Translated by Archbishop Joseph Cunnane, of Tuam, and revised by Michael Mooney and Enda Lyons of St. Jarlath's College, Tuam, County Galway. In *Vatican Council II.* Vol. 1, *The Conciliar and Post-Conciliar Documents.* Edited by Austin P. Flannery. Northport, NY: Costello Publishing Company, 1998.

Vaughn, David L. "Implementing Spirituality in Catholic Parish Councils." Thesis submitted in partial fulfillment of the requirements for certification in the National Association of Church Business Administration at the University of St. Thomas, St. Paul, MN, June, 1994.

Youngstown, Diocese of. *A Guide for Parish Pastoral Councils: A People of Mission and Vision* (2000). Available at http://www. doy.org/parish2000.PDF (accessed April 27, 2007).

Zech, Charles E., ed. *The Parish Management Handbook: A Practical Guide for Pastors, Administrators, and Other Parish Leaders.* See especially chap. 7, "Developing Stewards in a Parish Setting." Mystic, CT: Twenty-Third Publications, 2003.

Zech, Charles E., and Mary L. Gautier, Robert J. Miller, and Mary E. Bendyna, RSM. *Best Practices of Catholic Pastoral and Finance Councils.* Huntington, IN: Our Sunday Visitor Publishing Division, 2010.